Was It Something I Said?

Also by Jess McCann

You Lost Him at Hello: From Dating to "I Do" - Secret Strategies from One of America's Top Dating Coaches

Was It Something I Said?

THE ANSWER TO ALL
YOUR DATING DILEMMAS

Jess McCann

Guilford, Connecticut
An imprint of Globe Pequot Press

skirt!® is an attitude . . . spirited, independent, outspoken, serious, playful and irreverent, sometimes controversial, always passionate.

To buy books in quantity for corporate use
or incentives, call **(800) 962-0973**
or e-mail **premiums@GlobePequot.com.**

Project editor: Meredith Dias
Text Design: Sheryl P. Kober
Layout artist: Maggie Peterson

Library of Congress Cataloging-in-Publication Data

McCann, Jess.
  Was it something I said? : the answer to all your dating dilemmas / Jess McCann.
     p. cm.
  ISBN 978-0-7627-8209-3
  1. Dating (Social customs) 2. Man-woman relationships. 3. Single women—Psychology. I. Title.
  HQ801.M4848 2013
  306.7—dc23
                    2012025900

Printed in the United States of America

10 9 8 7 6 5 4 3 2 1

To my husband, Erik,

I hope every woman finds a man as
wonderful as you.

Contents

Contents

Contents

Introduction

IN LOVE AND TONGUE-TIED

I had just cuddled up on the couch with a good book when my phone rang on a Tuesday night. It was one of my clients, Charlotte, who was supposed to be out on a first date.

"Charlotte, what happened? Why aren't you on your date?" I asked.

I could barely hear Charlotte's reply as she whispered, "I *am* on my date. I'm calling you from the bathroom!"

I sat up on the couch and put down my book. Was the date that bad? Did she need me to rescue her?

"Is everything okay? Is it not going well?" I asked.

"No, that's not it. It's going extremely well! I like him a lot. We're having a great time," she assured me.

"That's great," I said. "So why are you in the bathroom calling me and not out there having dinner?"

"I don't want to screw this up," Charlotte declared. "I really like him, and I'm afraid I'm going to say or do something wrong," she said in a panic.

"Just relax," I told her. "You'll be fine. You're ready to meet someone grea, and you're not going to screw this up."

Charlotte breathed a bit easier. "Thanks. I needed to hear that. But I do have one question for you, and it's the reason I'm calling."

"Sure, what is it?" I asked.

"He asked me if I was dating anyone else, and I'm not sure what to say. This is a first date, so wouldn't it be okay if I said I was dating other people? I don't want him to think I have trouble getting dates. At the same time, if I say I'm seeing someone he may take that as me allowing him to do the same, and I don't want him going out with other women. I know I may be reading too much into this, but I don't want to say the wrong thing and ruin my chances with the best guy I've met in a long time!"

Charlotte was talking so fast I could hardly keep up with her.

"Just take a deep breath, Charlotte. If he asks you if you're seeing anyone else, smile at him and just say, 'not exclusively,'" I advised. "You don't have to dive into any details. Just keep it short and simple."

"Not exclusively! That's perfect. Thank you, Jess!" she said, relieved. "I am so thankful you answered your phone. I will say just that. Not exclusively. Thank you, again," Charlotte said. And with that she hung up the phone and hurried back to her date.

That was around seven-thirty. At quarter to ten, my phone rang again.

"Charlotte?" I said.

"Jess! Oh, thank you for answering again. I'm sorry for calling, but I have another question," she stammered.

"Okay," I said. "Are you still on your date?" She didn't sound like she was in the bathroom this time.

"Yes, I'm still with him. He's bringing the car around. He asked me if I wanted to go to a movie with him tomorrow. I know I should say no because, as you've said, I need to build anticipation. So how do I turn him down but still let him know I want to go out with him again? What should I say?" she asked in a hurry.

"Tell him you would love to go to a movie, but tomorrow you have plans. Don't specify what they are. Then ask if there is another day that works," I told her.

"Thank you again, Jess! I didn't know what to say exactly. That's perfect though. Have a great night, and I will talk to you soon." Charlotte hung up quickly.

She called two more times after that.

If we haven't met before, my name is Jess McCann and I'm a dating coach. Women from all over the world contact me to discuss their love lives. I started this business several years ago when I had a remarkable awakening about dating, an awakening that changed me from a desperately seeking single girl to a happily married woman, and that inspired me to open my own coaching practice. You see, for most of my life, I didn't understand men and had trouble with relationships myself. I had a library of sob stories—from being dumped over e-mail to being stood up on my birthday. Then something miraculous happened that changed dating for the rest of my life. It all started when I landed my first job.

It wasn't just any job. It was a job in door-to-door sales, the lowest form of peddling you can imagine. At the time, I was twenty-two years old and at rock bottom of both my personal and professional life. My very recent ex-boyfriend had a new girlfriend, and as luck would have it, I ran into them everywhere. Besides being depressed and self-conscious, I was working on straight commission, which meant I was almost always broke. I thought life would never turn around for me. I swore I was

Introduction

doomed to wander the planet alone and dirt poor. I had no idea that just a few years later, life would change dramatically and lead me to a greater love than I ever imagined.

To escape my problems at the time, I threw myself into work and decided to start my own sales company. As I trained my four-person sales staff to go door-to-door pitching products, I began to rebuild my own shattered self-confidence. With each deal I closed, I strengthened my people skills. I learned how to relate to my buyers and ultimately win them over. My sales team quickly expanded, and within months we became one of the top producing businesses of our kind.

It was during this time that I had my awakening.

One night after work, I was set up on a date. As I sat there chatting with the guy over some shared calamari, I found myself more confident and self-assured than I had ever been before. In a sudden "aha" moment, I realized that all my job training had not only helped me become a better salesperson, it had helped me become a better, more confident version of myself. Every customer call had taught me how to build a rapport with someone. I had essentially learned the fundamental do's and don'ts of relationship building hands on. I knew how to get people interested in what I had to say; I knew how to keep them interested and secure a commitment. It never dawned on me that the skills I had learned would benefit my personal life, but that is just what happened. I no longer felt confused or anxious around men. I had unknowingly and unintentionally learned to handle romantic relationships through my business. The dark cloud had finally lifted, and for the first time in my life I felt in control of my destiny.

After that, the tables turned for good. I was no longer the one stewing and stressing over guys. They were the ones now worrying about me. The gender-wide problem of where to meet single men disappeared. I met them everywhere: in bars and restaurants, in coffee shops and grocery stores. The recurring setbacks I had in the past vanished. I was dating in a completely different way than I ever had before. In fact, dating itself became fun and enjoyable.

Then one night, while I was out prospecting with some friends, I saw a very cute guy and asked if I could borrow his menu. His name was Erik, and I was immediately taken with him. He was everything I had been searching for my whole life. We fell in love and married two years later. As cliché as it sounds, I truly feel like I am now the luckiest and happiest woman on earth.

In 2007 I started my personal date coaching business and the next year penned my first book to teach single women how to change their dating destiny just as I had. I revealed all the techniques to find a guy, get him interested, and keep him that way. *You Lost Him at Hello: A Saleswoman's Secret to Closing the Deal with Any Guy You Want* hit bookshelves and immediately went to work helping women across the country. Almost instantly I began receiving e-mails from readers everywhere. Women of all ages were seeing immediate results, and even a number of men were benefiting from the advice. Both began meeting people with much greater ease. Many had realized their bad dating habits and were now able to avoid the big relationship pitfalls. But most important, a great many of them were getting into happy, healthy relationships.

There was still one thing that troubled me, however. Regardless of how much their love lives had improved, some women still encountered daily hiccups that easily threw them off course. Answering a seemingly simple text message became a monumental source of stress and could often completely derail them. *You Lost Him at Hello* had provided an all-over dating strategy that allowed women to jump-start more potential relationships. Now what they needed were tactics. The countless letters I received contained long, sometimes complicated questions seeking specific situational advice on how to communicate with a guy in the best possible way. Several book fans told me, for instance, that they loved the concept of ending their dates at the *Height of Impulse* (which means to end your night when you feel your date is having the most fun with you, and not when he or she is tired and ready to go home), but they were not sure how to best execute this, specifically on a first date. One reader told me she agreed that she needed to go home instead of back to her date's apartment, but she didn't quite know how to tell her date that! She was afraid of coming off as disinterested by turning him down and worried he wouldn't call her again. Much like my client Charlotte, she wanted to know exactly what to say and how to say it.

Some women would write to me and tell me they had already made a mistake, and wondered what they could say or do to salvage things. They felt paralyzed with fear of making the wrong decision and needed guidance. When the pressure mounted, many of them either became tongue-tied or put their foot in their mouth, which frequently made matters worse. Their queries flooded my in-box daily. Was it possible to turn a one-night stand into a real relationship, or did they need to accept the error of their ways and move on? Could you get someone who's lost interest in you re-interested? What could you say or do to turn things around? But for the most part, the majority of e-mails posed common everyday questions that inevitably popped up at some point because of the world we live in today. With my coaching clients, we had time to drill down into the particulars of each situation. I was always on hand to help steer them in the right direction and help them craft an appropriate reply. With the high volume of reader questions pouring in every day, though, I couldn't address them all despite my best efforts. That is why I decided to write this book.

Most of us stumble through our relationships, forced to learn through trial and error. We consult our friends, family, and even the great and powerful Google for solemn advice, so that we don't make a misstep and unwittingly sabotage our chances at happiness. But what if we could all learn from one another's relationships instead of trying to figure things out on our own? The one thing I know for certain is no matter how different, how complicated, or how enormous or minute a problem may be to someone, there are a million other people around the world in the exact same predicament. In the pages that follow, I've compiled questions from women (and a few men) around the globe, searching for answers to the most common yet complex dating scenarios.

Maybe you have a general grasp of the big do's and don'ts of dating, but it's those little glitches that end up throwing you off course and causing your relationship to crash. Perhaps you know what you are supposed to do, but you just can't figure out how or when to do it. Or maybe you just continually find yourself always saying the wrong thing, which unintentionally ruins your romantic opportunities. This book can help with all of that.

Although we can't control someone's behavior, we *can* control the way in which we respond to it. What you may not realize is that much of what you *say* to someone is communicated in your actions and inactions as much as it is in the actual words you speak. Sometimes the most powerful point you can make can be communicated without even uttering a word. Reacting in the most appropriate way and choosing the most well-suited verbiage can often defuse or redirect an awkward or fatal situation. Relationships are not perfect, and there will always be moments of strife and uncertainty, so learning how to handle mishaps and setbacks can mean the difference between parting ways or patching things up. In this book you will find techniques you may recognize from *You Lost Him at Hello* applied in situations you may not have thought of before. You will also be introduced to new techniques derived from my experience both as a dating coach and as a sales manager. You will learn how to handle yourself when uncomfortable scenarios arise, how to make often agonizing discussions go smoothly, and when it is best to speak up versus letting your silence do the talking for you.

If you have ever had a conversation with someone you like suddenly snowball out of control, then this is the book for you. If you have ever been at a loss for words or said something you've regretted later, I can help. Learning just how to approach a delicate situation can take years of practice, and dating situations are always delicate. But the following pages will help you approach these situations and get you to a better place, faster. It will answer all your dating questions and give you play-by-play instructions on how to best address each problem.

Ladies, while you read, keep in mind that the primary intent isn't to simply conquer every man you're after and lock him into a relationship just because you can. Instead, your goal should be to keep him interested long enough for you to evaluate the most critical element of a happy, healthy relationship: determining whether he is not only *the right person* for you but *a good person* in general. If he's not a man of good character, then no matter what you do or say, chances are your relationship will always be turbulent. While this book will help identify those qualities in a man and guide you through tough times and awkward situations, there may be little remedy if you settle on a partner who lacks the values that are truly needed for a good partnership. This book provides you with the recipes for relationship success. However, it will work only if you come to the table with the right ingredients.

Chapter One

TEXTING AND CALLING

In 1997, I was a sophomore in college. My roommate transferred to another school halfway through the year, and I was left living alone in our dorm. At that time, I had just started to take an interest in a well-known soccer player named Chris. I had met him at a party, and he had asked for my number. Three days later, which would be seven years in girl time, he still hadn't called and I remember wondering if he ever would.

I recall coming home one night that week around eleven after studying with some friends in the University Center. When I walked in the door, I noticed the blinking light on my answering machine, indicating I had a new message. Oh, how that light made me light up. I hit the play button and eagerly waited to hear who had left the message. It was Chris. The time stamp was 4:18 p.m. He was calling to say hello and asking to get together that weekend. He laughed and admitted that he had called me the day before but didn't leave a message. He left his number and said he hoped to hear from me soon. I went to bed that night with a smile on my face and Chris's number on my corkboard.

When I called back the next day, Chris said he was happy to hear from me. He surprisingly admitted that he was worried that *I* had forgotten all about *him!* We got together for dinner and a movie that weekend.

Well, that weekend turned into the next weekend, and the weekend after that. Soon we were seeing each other on a regular basis. He took me to his fraternity formal. I introduced him to my parents. We spent a wonderful summer together filled with many of the late-night philosophical conversations that college so often seems to cultivate. After school ended we parted ways, but it was a good relationship that resulted in a lasting friendship.

If I were in college now, this story would have probably played out very differently. Let's go back to that voice mail.

As I said before, I waited three days for Chris to call. He did call on the second day—but I didn't know about it. Today, that would never have happened. His number would have popped up on my caller ID if I'd had a landline, but more than likely it would have been tracked on the cell phone resting safely in my purse pocket. If Chris had left a message today at 4:00 p.m., I wouldn't have had to wait until I returned home hours later to hear it. That's the beauty of mobile phones. No more waiting. No more wondering. No more mysterious missed calls.

But here's the not-so-beautiful part. Back in 1997, Chris felt like I was elusive and unattainable because for three days he could not reach me. After leaving me a message at four in the afternoon, he then had to wait around for me to call him back the next day (because eleven o'clock was too late to call someone's house). This waiting game was a natural course of action for decades and played a key part in building anticipation to see someone.

Today, however, we live in a world of instant gratification. There is no anticipating his call or, even more important, him anxiously awaiting your call back. If a guy calls you at four and you miss it, you may hold out for an hour, but, let's be honest, what kind of buildup is that? In many ways, our cell phones have become our own worst enemies. With instant messaging and constant texting, how can anyone play hard to get? If you think dating was easier ten or fifteen years ago, you're right. Communication was limited, which forced us to abide by certain rules. These rules benefited us, creating an illusion of unavailability. Now we are unrestricted. We can track down anyone at the push of a button, and most of us are taking full advantage—regardless of the long-term consequences. In the good old days, a man typically had to wait a full twenty-four to forty-eight hours to hear back from you, and in some cases, even longer. What if you were on vacation? Or you had company in town? You had to wait until you were home, where it was nice and quiet, to make that return call. Nowadays, you could be standing in line at a Starbucks in New Zealand. If you have been waiting for his call, chances are you will take it any time, any place. Most women say they can't help it. They fear if they don't pick up the phone or respond quickly, the guy will either get mad, lose interest, or move on to someone else. Some women worry about seeming rude or manipulative, and others just simply find it too emotionally difficult to hold out on calling back. No matter what your reason is, it will never be valid enough to ward off the inevitable: That which makes you more available will also make you less desirable. Think about that the next time you struggle with calling or texting back.

No woman wants to play games, but unfortunately now is not the time to hang up your cleats. With iPhones and BlackBerries working against us, you have no choice but to play another round.

Dating is delicate in the beginning, and a man's interest can wax and wane, so knowing how to handle a simple thing like text messaging is of vital importance. You may think you are making an insignificant move when you text, but don't let the simple gesture fool you. It's a small act that carries big weight. Knowing how to handle certain text-related situations could make or break the future of your relationship. How long should you wait to text a guy back? Is there a way to get him to actually call instead? What if he only wants to "sext" with you? Can you get him to stop and ask you out on a proper date?

The following questions are the most frequent texting problems we face today, with detailed advice on how to manage them.

Should I Text Him First? What Should I Say?

Dear Jess,

While I was out with some friends, I met a very cute and funny guy! We flirted with each other all night, and just before he left he gave me his number and told me to call him. I don't know why he didn't ask for my number instead. Should I be texting or calling him first? I don't even know what I would say!

Whenever possible, you should avoid being the first one to make contact, whether by text or any other modern-day device. It is important to let the guy make the first move, just to make sure that he is genuinely interested in you. However, if a guy arms you with his number and requests that you call him, don't panic. This could easily be his way of letting you know he'd like to see you again, without him having to open himself up for rejection.

Asking for your number would require you to accept or reject him on the spot (and to his face). Telling *you* to call *him* allows a guy to walk away with his dignity intact. If you choose not to contact him afterward, the sting of rejection from a *Silent No* is much less painful.

If a guy suggests you call him, the first thing you have to do is analyze his interest, or what I refer to as *Buying Signs*. You don't want to call a guy who only gave you his number because he had no other way to end the conversation. Determine his level of interest by examining a few key signals. Did he approach you and proceed to flirt with you all night? Did he make any physical contact (touch your arm or shoulder)? Was he maintaining strong eye contact while asking you questions about yourself? If so, then it's a good sign he really wants to hear from you. Go ahead and make the first move this time. Enjoy the power that is now in your hands. Preparing for a voice-on-voice conversation can be a little overwhelming, so dial it down a notch and opt for a simple text message. You could either text him something cheeky like, *Here's my #... use it at your own risk ;-)*. Or you could send him something more personal pertaining to the conversation you had the night you met. I would not send him a *Hey it's me, from the bar the other night* text. A message like that doesn't convey much confidence. It will be perceived as if you expected him to have forgotten all about you. Assume he's been waiting by the phone ever since he gave you his number. After all, why wouldn't he be?

Once you decide what to say, you will then have to determine when the best time is to make contact. Even though you have downgraded to the most casual form of communication, even a small five-worded text can have a big impact. Knowing that, you should err on the side of caution. Text too soon, and you can scare a guy off. But text too late, and if he is truly interested, he still will reply to your message. Therefore, play it safe and use the two-day rule. A great deal of the male population follows this rule religiously and for the most part it works well. Why try to reinvent the wheel? If he gives you his number on Saturday night, wait forty-eight hours, and text him on Monday. The only exception to this rule is if you met him two days before the weekend. You don't ever want to send a first text on a Friday or Saturday. You are too busy doing other things, of course! So if you met him on Thursday, you should wait until Sunday evening or Monday.

How Long Should I Wait to Return a Text?

Dear Jess,

Last week I gave a guy my number. It took him six days to contact me, but he finally sent me a text. How long do I have to wait to respond to him?

You will more likely find yourself in this situation than the one before, but don't think that because you are merely responding to him this time, you don't have to put in as much thought.

I'm a fan of applying old-school rules to new technology, so the first time a guy reaches out to you, you should wait at least twenty-four hours to respond. It does not matter if he texts, calls, e-mails, or instant messages. Whatever mode of communication he chooses still warrants the same reply time. Having difficulty with that? Think of it this way: Ever since you gave him your number six days ago, you've been staring at your phone, recapping the night you met him, second-guessing his interest, and

Was It Something I Said?

undoubtedly doubting yourself, *what has he been doing?* Going to the gym, seeing his friends, and, oh yeah, not calling you. As you've been sitting there in a quiet panic, wondering if you were going to hear from him, he's been living life worry free. Now that he's called you, it's his turn to wait and stress a little. However, if you call or text him back immediately, that won't happen. If he actually calls you, do not pick up. Let your voice mail handle things for now and return his call the following day. This isn't revenge for making you wait—it's just rebalancing for the greater good of your future relationship.

After you text him back the first time, you are going to have to vary your response tactics. If you religiously wait exactly twenty-four hours each time, he will eventually pick up on your pattern and think you are playing a game. It's always a good idea to let time pass before you reciprocate a call or text, but if you want to remain a mystery and keep the chase going, the key is to *be unpredictable*. Text back immediately some of the time but then wait a few hours or a whole day the next. Keep him on his toes by being unpredictable when it comes to your return texts and calls.

What If He Calls and Doesn't Leave a Message?

Dear Jess,
    Update! He just called! But for some reason he didn't leave a message. Can I call him back?

If you want a guy to know that you have been sitting by the phone eagerly awaiting his call, then by all means, go right ahead and call him back. But consider this first: How do you know that he really meant to call you and this wasn't just an accidental pocket dial? How embarrassed will you be if you call him and he says that he didn't really intend to call you? Then all that self-restraint you've been exercising will be for nothing. He'll think, "Wow, I pocket-dialed her and she got so excited she called me!"

For argument sake, let's say he did purposefully call you and did not leave a voice mail; if you call him back, you will be setting a precedent that he doesn't ever have to leave you a message. While you may not care about that right now because you are so elated to hear from him, you will care after it happens for the tenth or fifteenth time. He will learn that he can do the bare minimum, and you will still jump to his attention. In essence, you are positively reinforcing bad manners and unconsciously telling him that you aren't worthy of being properly pursued.

One of my clients constantly struggled with her phone etiquette, too. She would always answer when a guy would call and promptly returned texts no matter what time of day. Eventually men stopped leaving her voice mails because they knew they didn't need to put in the extra effort. I tried to explain to my client that she needed to break her bad habit, but she would argue that because guys knew she had a cell phone, if she didn't reply quickly, they would assume she was playing games and get annoyed with her. The irony was that men seemed to get annoyed with her anyway. She was never properly asked out on a date and had a hard time turning the few first dates that she did get into second dates. After reaching her wits' end, I convinced her to try to reform her ideas on mobile communication. Guess what happened? More guys called, more left messages, and more asked her for second dates.

In your case, the best thing to do is ignore that missed call. Don't send your guy a text asking if he called, or reach out to him in any other way. Remember that men *want to* pursue women, so allow him to do just that. If you take that away from him in the beginning, he will lose interest. And who knows, maybe he didn't leave a message because he wanted to call you back in the hopes of reaching you on the phone.

What If He Texts Me Right Away?

Dear Jess,

I met a guy out one night and he texted me before I even got home. He just said it was nice meeting me and that he wanted me to have his number. Do I still wait to text back?

You can text him that very night; however, by doing so, you are putting yourself into a much more casual zone. If you want this guy to ask you on a date, you need to do what's smart, no matter how excited you are over him, or how simple the text message may be.

A client of mine named Krista never had trouble meeting men, but she had a tough time getting them to actually ask her out. They would contact her all hours of the day but made no mention of planning a date. When we looked at her patterns, the problem was obvious. She would respond immediately after a guy's initial text, which usually occurred just hours after they had first met. This allowed the guys to get too comfortable, too soon. Instead of being asked out to dinner, Krista was often sent the "meet up" text, suggesting she come out and meet the guy with his friends, usually at a bar or club somewhere. It wasn't until she stopped the casual contact that she saw better results.

If you give a guy your number and he immediately sends you a "Nice meeting you text," at least wait until the next day to reply. You don't have to apologize for not responding sooner. You were out, busy with your friends, having a good time, or home in bed relaxing. Remember, he is just a random guy to you at the moment. He is not your top priority, nor does he want to be right now. The day after he texts, get up and go about your business. Then when lunchtime rolls around, send him a quick, "Nice meeting you too!" Don't attempt to continue the conversation by asking him any questions. If he wants to keep it going, he will. It may take him several hours or another whole day to respond after your text, but that is a good sign. It means based on your delayed response, he is carefully weighing his next move.

What I am about to say may sound sacrilegious, but it's imperative to understand that not all texts require a response. In fact, I encourage you to *only* answer texts from men when you are asked a question or when closing out a conversation. So, in many cases, the guy should be the last one to text you.

My client Vanessa has had a hard time adhering to this guideline. Recently she went out with a bunch of coworkers and met a handsome friend of a friend. They exchanged numbers and Vanessa was hopeful the guy would ask her on a date. The day after they met, Vanessa sent out a mass text to everyone saying she had a great time and wished everyone a good upcoming week. The guy responded to her text with, "Thanks! It was definitely a fun night. Hope you have a good week, too."

In this instance, Vanessa should have not responded to that text. The guy had replied to her initial message but did not continue the conversation by asking her any questions. In fact, he blatantly closed the conversation out. By not texting back, their communication would have been balanced. She would have sent *one* text to him and he would have sent *one* text back. But instead Vanessa replied, made reference to the guy's upcoming work trip, and wrote back, "Very fun! Hope you have a great flight tomorrow." The guy never responded.

Texting is not like playing tennis. You don't have to return his every serve to keep the game going. Men who are interested in you will not hesitate to text you twice in a row. If you've been accused of being overeager or you have lots of men texting you but few asking you out, I strongly suggest sticking to my text-back rule. Only text back when you are asked a question or if you are texted something that is meant to elicit a reaction from you. For instance "My car broke down on the highway" does not ask a question, but it certainly warrants a response.

Should I Send a "Thank You" Text after Our Date?

Dear Jess,

I'm worried that guys can't tell I'm interested and so don't ask for a second date . . . either that, or there's something else I'm doing that's putting them off because I don't get asked out twice. I'm also not sure if and when a post-date "thank you" text message is a good idea. I worry that if I don't send a follow-up note, I will be viewed as rude and ungrateful. What should I do?

Why do you think men don't know you are interested? You said yes to the date, didn't you? That alone is enough to reinforce your interest. It is possible, however, that all the worrying you are doing is giving off an undesirable vibe. *The key ingredient for a great first date is being relaxed and having fun.* That is what it is all about in the beginning. You should be laughing and enjoying each other's company as you get to know each other, not stressing about how much interest to show or what you should do postdate. If you want to go on a second date, don't overthink the first one. Show interest by being there, being engaged, and having a good time. If you feel worried, stressed, or anxious, the guy will absolutely sense it.

To fight those pesky nerves and demonstrate just the right amount of interest, use the *Mirror Theory* and imitate his behavior. The *Mirror Theory* advocates that you take interest cues from your date and reciprocate the same amount back to him. Smile when he smiles, laugh when he laughs, and lean in to him when he leans in to you. Mirror his body language and tone, and you will be sure to show him the perfect level of interest because it will be mirroring his. Most women who worry like you end up showing too much interest and giving off the perception they want to hop into a relationship before the bill is even paid. Instead, listen to your date and mirror the affection he shows you. For example, if he pays you a compliment, return one to him. If he holds the door for you, mirror his gesture with the right response. Look him right in the eye, smile, and give him a sincere thank you. Trust that the mirror theory will show just the right amount of interest to get you that next date.

As for sending him that "thank you" text . . . don't do it. Like we've discussed before, cell phones are a relatively new device in the grand scheme of relationships. People have been dating for centuries without them. Even just looking back ten or fifteen years, if you wanted to tell a guy how much fun you had on your first date, you told him on your doorstep right before he kissed you goodnight. There were no cell phones, so there were no follow-up texts. However, more and more women these days consider it downright rude not to send a follow-up text after the guy has just taken them out. But just because the technology now exists, does that mean we have to use it? Men were getting along just fine for years without the additional "thank you again." You should absolutely show your gratitude for the good time he has shown you, but express it live and in person, not over the phone. Once the date is coming to an end, there are a variety of ways to let him know that you had fun and would like to see him again, without seeming overly eager. For tips on how to do this, go to page 54, *Do I Have to Kiss Him on a First Date?*

You don't want to tip your hand, but, even more so, you want to know *where you stand with him.* If anyone is going to follow up after a date, it should be the guy thanking you! If he sends you a post-date text, it's a huge *Buying Sign* that lets you know you will likely see him again. You won't have to sit around for days pondering if and when you will hear from him. If you get the follow-up text, it is a good indication that the second date won't be too far away.

Can I Send Him a Text If I Haven't Heard from Him in a While?

Dear Jess,

I had three amazing dates with a guy last month, but I haven't heard from him since! It's been over two weeks and I really want to see him. Can I send him a casual, "How are you?" text and see if that gets us reengaged?

If you had three amazing dates and this guy hasn't called you again, something has happened that a casual text won't fix.

Maybe an ex-girlfriend came back into his life, or perhaps he met someone else. Either way, your reaching out to him isn't going to change his feelings about you, and making the text "casual" won't cover up your true intentions. Men are perceptive, and he will undoubtedly know that "How are you?" really means, "Where have you been?"

Even if he left his baseball hat in your car or his sweater in your apartment, don't use that as an excuse to make contact. Again, "I have your baseball cap" really means "I want to see you." If you are looking for an excuse to contact him that seems reasonable and benign, there is none. He knows what you are doing and you are potentially setting yourself up for him to ask you to drop his hat off when he's not home.

If you absolutely *must* contact him because you cannot control yourself from doing otherwise, here is my best suggestion: Send him a text (or e-mail if that is your preferred method of communication) that says the following:

"Hey! Was just thinking about you and wanted to say hello. Hope you are having a good week."

Why is that the best thing to say? Because any text from you, regardless of content, indicates you were thinking about him, so you should own up to it instead of hiding behind his baseball hat. Second, this text makes you seem much more mature and confident in yourself, because you are being honest about your feelings without being overly effusive. Last, you aren't asking him any questions in this text. You are not requiring or pressuring or trying to illicit any response, which I know goes against why you were texting him in the first place, but in this situation he needs to text you back because he wants to and not because he feels obligated. If there is a sliver of hope left in this relationship,

Was It Something I Said?

he will take your bait and write back to you. Then you will know it will be because he respects you, not because he felt bad leaving you hanging.

A warning: Just because he does text back does not mean he is planning to ask you out again. If you think he's disappeared because you've done something to scare him off and want to correct your mistake, skip to page 106, *I Ruined My Chances with a Great Guy. Can I Win Him Back?*

How Can I Get Him to Initiate Contact?

Dear Jess,

I met someone two weekends ago who I really like. When we are together, we have a great time. The only problem is that I am always the one initiating contact. If I don't text him, I won't hear from him for days. How do I encourage him to make more of an effort?

It sounds like patience is a virtue that you may be lacking. If you started dating this guy only a couple of weeks ago, how often do you think he should be contacting you? Every day? Twice a day? I don't think you need to encourage him to text you any more frequently. Instead, I think you need to lower your "texpectations." Contacting you every two or three days is normal behavior for a guy at this stage. If he's smart, he's got his own strategy to win you over, too. It sounds like you grow impatient, however, and beat him to the punch. I will warn you that if you don't let this guy pursue you and stop texting him so often, he will lose interest. Relax, be patient, and let him reach out to you.

That said, after a couple of months, you should be talking via some form of communication almost every day, even if it's just a quick e-mail to say hello. The more a guy likes you, the more he's going to want to see and talk to you. If his contact does not increase or wanes over time, you should consider that a red flag that something is amiss. A sudden change in pattern usually indicates a problem. If you are doing all the initiating at this point, stop and see how long it takes your guy to reach out to you. If you go more than a week without hearing from him, he could be losing interest. You don't need to give up just yet, but you may need to reexamine your approach to this relationship. To figure out what to do next, jump to page 89, *Why Did My Boyfriend Suddenly Become Distant?*

How Do I Get Him to Stop "Sexting" and Ask Me on a Date?

Dear Jess,

I'm a gay male and I have a crush on this guy. We run in the same circle of friends and recently he's been contacting me a lot through text, but they are mostly dirty text messages. How do I get him to stop "sexting" me and ask me out on a proper date?

From the minute a guy meets you, he is learning things about you. Some things are trivial, like what movies you enjoy or what bands you like. Other things are more crucial, like how you value yourself and what you consider acceptable dating behavior. It's obvious how someone learns the former, but figuring out what you consider acceptable dating behavior can be a trial-and-error

Was It Something I Said?

process. If you have responded positively to his "sext" messages in the past by acknowledging them or indulging in them, he will continue his behavior because he sees it working for him. Even just replying with a "Lol" can lead him to believe that you are okay with this type of interaction.

Whether you are a man or a woman, if someone's rude, crude, or dirty texts are making you uncomfortable, the best response is always no response at all. This will send the message that you are owed more respect without directly having to call anyone out on their tactless text. You are not obligated to reply to a guy's every beck and call, therefore let the sext message hang out there in limbo. When he hasn't heard back from you in a while, he will recall the last exchange you had. When he sees it's his dirty text message, he will begin to realize he has crossed the line. Then, either let him text you again or, after some time has passed, text him with a complete change of subject. Eventually he will get the hint that this is not the way to win you over. You can't make him ask you out, but you can make him stop the sexting.

If he stops communicating because you've set this boundary, then understand that he is one of the few guys out there who doesn't have anything else in his repertoire than making sexual passes. There are some men who equate dirty to flirty and it's just their way of showing interest. This does not make it your job to compromise your comfort zone and simply put up with it. While you may like this guy and realize this is his rap, you also should be aware that he will most likely continue to communicate this way throughout the course of your relationship. Understand if you are having trouble connecting on a real, emotional level now, you will have just as hard of a time later. Don't think if you get through this one layer of tastelessness, a world of sensitivity and connectivity awaits you. Men put their best foot forward when they are first getting to know someone, so this is him at his best. Do not hold on to the hope that he will transform into a gentleman overnight. Some guys are just born and raised this way, and no matter what you do, nothing will change them. Accept him for who he is, or find someone with a little more depth and a lot more to offer you.

How Do I Get Him to Call Instead of Text?

Dear Jess,

A guy I met at a party texted me to ask me out on a first date. Don't guys usually call for that kind of thing? Does the fact that he texted me mean he's not that interested in me? I like hearing a guy's voice and I'm really starting to hate texting. How do I get a guy to pick up the phone and actually call?

As we've previously established, men prefer to be rejected via text than in person. Same rule applies here. He'd rather get a no response via text than hear you actually say the word *No*, or worse, *Who is this again?* Asking a woman out is a daunting task! Don't assume all men are made of steel. They have feelings too, and they fear rejection just as much as you do. Don't jump down his throat for asking you out over a text. It doesn't mean he's not that into you, and it doesn't mean he's *always* going to text you. As you get to know him, you will get a sense of his personality and habits. Sure, he could be texting you because he's lazy and uncommunicative, but it also could be because he is shy and sensitive. You won't know until you go out with him a few times and get to know him better. Some guys use texts because they have learned through

Was It Something I Said?

previous relationships that this is the best way to talk. Until you've spent some time with this person, you won't know if his aversion to voice-on-voice interaction is just a bad habit that needs breaking or if it is indicative of a more complex character flaw.

Which brings us to your second question: What can you do to persuade him to pick up the phone and actually call you? Many women have tried the direct approach. I had a friend who refused to communicate over text, and whenever a man attempted to have a conversation with her this way, she would text him, "I don't have text conversations. Pick up the phone and call me." Guess how many men followed her orders? Telling a man how to reach you isn't as effective as letting him learn for himself. Besides, you don't want to come off like my friend the Phone Nazi.

If you have had multiple, in-depth conversations over text with a guy, it's no wonder he hasn't called. You've taught him that this is the way you like to touch base, make plans, and catch up. To break this habit or, better yet, to prevent it from becoming one, use *The K.I.S.S Principle*. *The K.I.S.S. Principle* stands for *Keep It Short and Simple*. Saying too much and overexplaining oneself is a very common female problem. *The K.I.S.S. Principle* helps mitigate unintentional verbal vomit and, in this case, will also teach the guy he needs to call if he wants more conversation from you. Keep your texts very short and simple. Do not text long and lengthy messages, even if he does. If you are having a back-and-forth conversation, don't respond too quickly. Let him learn that if he wants an immediate response from you (which he does), he is better off calling.

If he doesn't take the hint, then look for the most opportune time to tell him you aren't a big texter. If you are out to dinner with your date and the subject of texting comes up, mention how terrible you are at it and how your friends and family all know that if they need you, they have to actually call you. Then ask him about his preferred method of communication. Does he like text, phone, or e-mail? Ask him in the same fun way you'd ask someone if they like red or white wine. Don't be too serious about it. Let him tell you why he likes to converse this way. He may tell you that he's surrounded by people at work or lives with a roommate and doesn't want him to overhear his conversation. You may be surprised that he has a valid reason for always texting.

A lot of the time this issue works itself out on its own. Texting is heavily embedded into our culture, so it's probably not that he's just not calling *you,* he's probably not calling his friends, family, and other people as well. Try to keep in mind that what is most important is how you are together. If the conversation flows easy on your dates, then I wouldn't worry so much about how he chooses to set them up. And if all else fails, you can always just tell him, "I'm over my texting limit for the month, so please just call me."

How Can I Get Him to Ask Me Out Instead of Just Texting Me?

Dear Jess,

Last month I met a guy through some mutual friends and we exchanged phone numbers. Since then he's been texting me all the time. Every day he sends me a "Good Morning Beautiful" text. The problem is he hasn't actually asked me out! He mentioned taking me to dinner the night we met but hasn't brought it up since. How much longer should I texually date him before giving up on him completely? He obviously likes me or he wouldn't be texting me. Is there anything I can do?

Was It Something I Said?

As much as I like the term "texually dating," you can't be dating someone you've actually never gone out with. It doesn't matter how beautiful he says you are or how many compliments he throws your way. *What matters here is what he is not saying.* And what he's not saying is, *will you go out with me?* Maybe he has a girlfriend you don't know about. Maybe he's not interested in dating you but likes the security of knowing you like him. Either way, if he isn't asking you out, he has a reason for it, and you should not put your dating life on hold hoping he makes a move.

The reason you are not going on real dates has nothing to do with you. There is something else going on in his life that is deterring him from moving forward with your relationship. However, there are a few things you can do in an attempt to push things along with this man if you aren't ready to give up on him completely. Either he will come around or he will back off, but you will make progress in one direction or another.

First, *become more unpredictable with your communication with him.* See if you can shake things up a bit. If you always text each other in the morning, start holding off your responses until the afternoon. If he senses that you are getting fed up with him, he may spring to action. Otherwise, depending on how bold you want to be, you can be honest and text him, "I am getting carpal tunnel from all this texting! We should have this conversation over coffee instead." Asking him out but keeping it light with coffee just may work.

A warning though: If you do suggest a coffee date, you should be prepared for the possibility of no response or an excuse not to meet you. If he has not asked you out yet, there is presumably a reason. When you put him on the spot and ask for the date, you will get an answer one way or another. Even if he doesn't respond to your request, *no answer is an answer!* For more insight into men who stay in contact without asking you out, jump to page 158, *We've Communicated for Months. Why Won't He Meet Me?*

How Do I Get Him to Stop Checking His Phone?

Dear Jess,

The guy I'm dating is always on his phone! He constantly checks his e-mail, and he is always texting his friends. It's so annoying. How do I get him to stop and pay more attention to me?

There is nothing attractive about a guy who is glued to his phone. What you should do here is determine the root of this problem. Is he just oblivious and doesn't realize his phone faux pas, or does this annoying habit run deeper than that? To find out, ask yourself this: Besides his phone addiction, is he also a bad listener? Does he seem to have a touch of A.D.D.? Does he get bored fairly quickly and always need to be in the thick of things? If you are nodding your head right now, then your problem isn't with this guy's phone, it's with this guy, and his phone fetish could be clueing you in on a bigger behavioral problem.

My client Natalie recently started dating the general manager at a very trendy D.C. restaurant. At first she found him exciting. He knew everyone in town and everyone knew him. But as they continued to date, she realized that his mind was *always* somewhere else. His phone was constantly ringing and he never failed to answer it, no matter where they were or what they were doing. He wanted to know what was going on in the city at all times. He told her it was for business purposes, but she couldn't quite grasp how partying until four in the morning would help a restaurant. Even on nights when nothing was happening and his phone was quiet, his mind would still be out on the town. Natalie eventually realized she could not have a relationship with someone who placed more value on life in the fast lane than spending quality time with her.

There is not much you can do if you are dating someone who lives in his own head. There are those types of guys out there who try so hard to be connected to everyone that they inevitably isolate themselves from a true connection with anyone. If this sounds like the person you are currently seeing, don't take it personally. He would act this way with any girl. It has nothing to do with you, and you shouldn't waste your time trying to change yourself because you think it will elicit more attention from him. The only thing to do is to move on to someone who knows the importance of being present to those people right in front of him.

However, if you think your guy is simply unaware of how often he's on the phone, *tell him how you feel,* but remain unemotional. If you start to get angry or frustrated, you will more than likely get push-back. Don't roll your eyes or give any other indicator that you are annoyed. Just tell him calmly that his phone use bothers you by using the words, "I feel." For example: "I notice you are on the phone a lot. *I feel* like this means you'd rather be out with your friends (or doing work)." Or if you have been dating for several months you can say: "When you are constantly checking your phone, I feel invisible and unimportant."

Most men will be quick to tell you that you are of the utmost importance, but don't stop at just reassurance. *Offer a solution to this problem.* If you have been together for only a few weeks, you have to make reasonable recommendations. For instance, if you usually meet him right after work, suggest meeting up an hour later, so he can have more time to himself to make calls. That is a reasonable solution. Do not suggest he turn off his phone at 8:00 p.m. sharp. You are not his mother, and you aren't in a position to make any demands. You need to speak your mind, but make sure the suggestion fits the situation. If you can't think of a good solution, ask him if he has one.

If he ignores your request to curtail his phone obsession or tells you that you are being unreasonable, jump to the Social Networking section of this book and turn to page 141, *Can I Tell My Boyfriend to Take Down Pictures of His Ex?* to learn what to do if a guy ignores your feelings when you've told him something is bothering you.

Should I Send Him a Nude Picture?

Dear Jess,

My boyfriend of three months recently asked me to send him a nude photo of myself. I told him I was worried about other people seeing it, but he promised he would never share it with anyone. I feel stuck! If I don't send him the picture, he will think I don't trust him. But if I do send it, I think I will regret it later. What do I do?

Trust your gut on this one. If you think you will regret it later, you most certainly will. I know your boyfriend says he won't show it to anyone, and right now he probably means it. But what happens if you break up? What happens if five years from now the relationship is ancient history, you've both moved on, but that picture is still stored in his phone or on his computer? In the grand scheme of things, this is a bad idea and even you know it. Tell your boyfriend this has absolutely nothing to do with trust. You know how easily pictures and videos can go viral, even by accident. What if someone else borrows his phone and flips through his photos? What if he loses his phone—or worse, someone steals it? Then that picture is in someone else's hands. Stand firm in your decision not to send the picture.

There are two ways to handle saying no to your man's request. First, you can take the direct approach and tell your boyfriend you won't be obliging him, using very assertive language. Here is what you should say: "I feel uncomfortable sending a picture like that over text (or e-mail), so I'm not going to send it to you. Sorry. I just have to do what feels right for me."

Do not say, "I don't want to send it . . . " because it leaves room for him to debate you. If you sound uncertain about your decision, he's likely to try to change your mind. Turning him down will disappoint him initially, but inwardly he will respect you for standing your ground.

If you are uncomfortable with the direct approach, there is another alternative. You can shift his focus by accommodating his request another way. If he's asking for the photo over text or e-mail, you can always write back, "I need to save something for when I see you in person." You can promise him a sexy striptease (as long as you are comfortable with it) or something else of equal interest. The most important thing here is that you don't succumb to pressure and that you stick to what you are okay doing.

What Can I Say to Those Guys Who Text and Then Disappear?

Dear Jess,

What about those guys who text you once and then when you text back they don't respond? Why even text you in the first place? Can you text them again and call them out for being jerks?

The text-then-no-text, as I like to call it, is a common complaint among the teen and twenties population, although it's never completely eradicated, even as people get older. (Sorry, ladies!) Contrary to popular belief, men will sometimes act on impulse and emotion without much deep thought into the future. In the case of the text-then-no-text, a guy can be craving some female attention and instinctively reach out and make contact. On your end, you may be thinking "Great! This guy likes me and we are going to start dating now!" because, unlike him, you are thinking about the future. He, however, is just taking care of an impulsive "itch" he is having in that moment. Regardless of the specific reason, that itch has now been scratched. To text this guy and tell him off would be in poor taste. He never promised that he would become your boyfriend or that he would even take you on a date. Can you really be angry and call someone out for not meeting your own built-up expectations?

One of my male clients had great insight into the text-then-no-text mystery. Aaron met a woman named Kate one night at a bar, and, after getting her phone number, he proceeded to text her the next day. He told her over text that it was wonderful talking with her and he hoped to take her out sometime soon. He also mentioned that he would give her a call on Sunday. That was the first and last text Aaron ever sent to Kate. He never followed up. From Kate's point of view, Aaron pulled a classic text-then-no-text and she would never know why he failed to call that weekend. Aaron, however, told me that although he thought Kate was attractive, he had been drinking heavily the night they met and could not remember how interested he truly was in her. He then got busy over the weekend and forgot to call. When Monday rolled around he considered calling Kate but still worried that his drinking thwarted his perception of her. What if she wasn't really as great as he remembered? What if she was like his needy ex-girlfriend? He decided to put off calling for another day or two, and before he knew it the end of the week had arrived. At that point Aaron decided he couldn't call Kate even if he wanted to because she would probably just hang up on him for waiting that long.

Most men are being sincere when they promise to call—at least at that moment. Aaron meant it when he said it as well; he just happened to talk himself out of it as the days rolled by. But Aaron had also recently broken up with a woman who was very clingy, and the fact that he wasn't quite ready to start dating again also played a part in his disappearing act.

When you get the text-then-no-text, one thing is clear. The guy is not (yet) serious about dating you. He may be wrapped up in work, friends, another girl, or a variety of other distractions. He had a life before he met you, and that life is the priority for now. Although you may be ready and available to start a new relationship, he may not be. Although you may want to start dating, he may have other plans. It's understandably confusing when a guy initiates a conversation with you and then doesn't move the relationship forward, but the bottom line is that he was just doing what felt right to him in the moment, and now that moment has passed. Don't beat yourself up trying to figure out what happened. Think more about the guys who *are* calling you, and forget about the ones who are not.

If, on the other hand, he did actually ask you out on a date, but then disappeared on you, jump to page 135, *Should I De-friend Him?*, to find out why he asked you out but never followed through.

Texting is more than a craze. It's typically the first form of communication among men and women, and it's here to stay (at least until it's upgraded). Guys rely heavily on texting, so like it or lump it, you will be sending and receiving a few hundred per relationship. Figuring out when and what to text can be a source of stress. But remember you are not a doctor on call. You are a single lady, hoping to fall in love. You are an independent woman with a life and a career, and to respond fast and frequently to a man you have just met or recently began dating would tell him he is more important than anything else in your world. You want to convey that you are confident, self-assured, and leading a life of fulfillment. To be a slave to your phone would contradict this. Bottom line: Sending him the right text is not as important as sending him the right message!

Chapter Two

DATING

"I think women should be heavily pursued and properly courted. A man should call, not text. He should pick me up, not ask me to meet him. He should arrange dinner at an upscale establishment. No chain restaurants. And he should always bring something for me. Flowers, or a bottle of wine at the very least. I don't think I'm asking for anything out of the ordinary. This is how my father pursued my mother, and how his father pursued my grandmother," Margot said quite frankly.

The twenty-six-year-old sitting in front of me was more refined than most. She was impeccably dressed, complete with Chanel suit and Manolo halter-back heels. She sounded confident to the untrained ear, but I had seen this type of woman before. That well-polished exterior and staunch set of rules on dating etiquette meant only one thing: She didn't have a clue what she was doing.

"When I'm not pursued correctly," she continued, "I lose interest, assuming the guy isn't that into me. But from what I know, when you don't seem interested, men try harder to keep you."

"Is that what you've found? That the less interested you are, the more men pursue you?" I asked.

Suddenly she let out a frustrated sigh. "No, it's not, and I'm not sure why. I know that I'm doing everything right. I'm smart, well educated, and attractive—I have good friends and a great job. I just can't seem to figure out why I'm still single. My other friends don't have this problem. I'm not sure why I do," she cried.

This is why people come to see me. Like twenty-six-year-old Margot, they want to be married, or at least seriously dating someone. They believe they are doing everything right, but there is something that is holding them back, and they can't figure out what it is. After asking their family, friends, and even their therapist, they end up here, hoping I will help solve their own mystery.

"I'm venturing a guess that you don't go on a whole lot of second dates?" I asked.

Margot shook her head. "I recently went out with a guy that I thought had real potential. We went out on a first date and he said he would call me to set up the next. He didn't call for three days. When he asked to see me again, I told him I was busy and all he said was, 'Oh, okay,' and quickly got off the phone. That was it. I never heard from him again."

"You said you were busy? Did you suggest another day to go out?" I asked.

"No, I just said I was busy. He had waited three days to call. I figured I had to communicate to him that it was inappropriate to wait that long."

"I think you communicated that pretty well," I said, "But were you interested only in making that point, or did you want to see him again?"

"Of course I wanted to see him again. I liked him. I can't believe he didn't want to see me again!"

I scratched my head in confusion. "But, Margot, he *did* want to see you again. He called and asked you out."

"Yes, three days later!" she practically shouted.

I began to see the problem. Margot had strict expectations in her head. She lived by certain rules that she assumed all men were aware of. She believed it was disrespectful to be called three days after a first date. She genuinely felt that if her date liked her more, he would have asked her out sooner. She assumed her rules were the rules everyone else abided by, and that thought alone was keeping her single.

"Margot, while women spend ample amounts of time reading, watching, and discussing the dynamics of a relationship, most men do not. They don't solicit advice from friends and family as we do. They often act off instinct, or past experience, but mainly they take their cues from you, the woman. They see how you react to them and adjust their strategy accordingly. When you said you were busy and offered no other positive reinforcement, like suggesting another day to meet, your date assumed you were not interested in seeing him again and dejectedly backed away," I explained.

"But, I'm not supposed to ask him out. He has to ask me. Besides, wouldn't a real man have kept trying?" she countered.

"A real man? No," I said. "A fool? Yes. If you don't know someone very well, and they respond negatively to you, why would you continue to assert yourself? Had you said no and suggested getting together another time, he would have known you wanted to see him again. However, you didn't do that. He's not a mind reader, Margot. No man is. They go only by your words and actions. Any thoughts or motivations behind them are easily misunderstood."

Margot slumped back in her chair.

"This is a lot harder than I expected. I guess I'm not sure how to show a guy interest without looking desperate," she said.

I closed my notebook and smiled at her. "It's a fine balance. The good news is that if you are willing to let go of your prior expectations, you can learn."

Dating is delicate; two people with different personalities, different backgrounds, different friends, and different experiences come together for the purpose of potentially forming a bond for the rest of their lives. Assumptions can be easily made; misunderstandings can undoubtedly happen. This is why there is so much riding on the first few dates. You don't know each other well enough to completely and accurately comprehend each other. As a woman you want to appropriately represent yourself while showing enough interest so he will know you like him, but not such an overabundant amount that it will scare him off. For the most part, being yourself is the best advice, but there are some situations that arise on dates that can easily thwart things, causing you to unintentionally distort your true self, your interest, or both. In this chapter we will discuss what is considered safe date conversation and how to answer first-date questions that may otherwise make you squeamish. We will strategize how to say yes to a man's short-notice invite without seeming too eager and what to say to a guy if you aren't ready to start smooching but he is.

The following are the most frequently fumbled dating scenarios with detailed advice on how to handle each in the best way.

Was It Something I Said?

How Should I End My Dates So He Stays Interested?

Dear Jess,

I've recently learned by reading *You Lost Him at Hello* that I should be ending my dates at the *Height of Impulse*. I'll admit I have not done this. My question is, how do I end the date at the *Height of Impulse* but still let the guy know I am interested? Won't he think if I am going home early, it means I don't like him?

When you are having fun on a date, the last thing you want to think about is going home, but allowing the evening to carry on for several hours (or in extreme cases, overnight) *severely* diminishes your chances at a long-term relationship. If you want to turn this hot new affair into a full-on commitment, you must have the courage to end your date at the *Height of Impulse*.

Ending your date at the *Height of Impulse* means that you say goodnight at a point in the evening when things are going well. Naturally, if both of you are having fun and really clicking, you won't want the date to end, but that is the very moment you need to part ways. Doing so will leave your guy wanting more of you and better your chances of getting another date.

After dinner, your date may try to take you to a second location to have a few more drinks, or he may even suggest going back to his place. You already know that you shouldn't oblige but worry about hurting his feelings if you decline. What if he takes it as a sign of rejection and never calls you again? How do you tell your date goodnight when he doesn't want you to leave yet?

Here is the perfect opportunity to use *Build–Break–Build*. *BBB* is a method commonly used to deliver unpleasant news. First, build him up by telling him what a wonderful time you had. Then you give him the break; you have to get home. Then you build him back up again to leave him on a positive note. Here's how you put it to action:

- Build: I had a great time tonight. The food was almost as good as the company. (Say this with a smile.)
- Break: It's getting late, so I better say goodnight now.
- Build: But this has been so much fun. I didn't realize you were such a funny guy [or insert any other adjectives that describe your date].

You can use the *Build–Break–Build* technique in any scenario where you need to turn down a guy gently. It will work wonders if you need to break or postpone a date, if you are asked to spend the night, or if he tries to get you to go away on a trip with him too soon. Keep your reason for turning him down short and simple (*K.I.S.S.*), and put more emphasis on your build. Although you may feel the urge, you don't have to elaborate on the break.

What Should I Do If We Are Long-distance Dating?

Dear Jess,

What do I do in instances where I am dating someone who doesn't live in my area and I'm not able to end my dates at the *Height of Impulse*?

Distance really throws a wrench into any potential relatio[n]
Because you cannot date at a graduated pace, when you do se[e]
guy you are apt to spend as much time with him as possible. You
may think it will all balance out because you won't see him again
for a while. However, if he returns home tired of you, you may not
see him again, period. A client of mine learned this the hard way.

Arielle, who is twenty-five, met Jeb on a girl's trip to Miami
Beach. They were both from cities in Pennsylvania, but the cities
were more than two hours away from each other. Arielle and Jeb
decided that even though the distance would be tough, they liked
each other enough to try to make it work. When they returned
home they spent a lot of time on Skype, and soon they planned a
trip for Jeb to stay with Arielle for three days.

The first several hours of the trip went really well. Arielle and
Jeb went out to dinner and had a lot of fun kissing and playing
footsy under the table. (This would be the *Height of Impulse.*) They
continued with a heavy make-out session back at Arielle's apartment and finally passed out around 3:00 a.m.

The next morning, Arielle, who is a big morning person,
made some coffee and turned on the TV. Jeb, who typically slept in
until ten on the weekends, was a little annoyed at this. They had
decided the night before to go to Longwood Gardens that day, but
Jeb was slow moving, and because they had drunk so much the
night before, said he would prefer just hanging in and watching
some football. Arielle immediately felt let down and upset. She
began making other suggestions for things they could do together,
but Jeb wasn't interested and he became irritated at her persis-
tence. After spending all day in front of the TV, they finally left the
house to grab some dinner. After downing a cheesesteak and fries,

Jeb's hangover had worn off and he was now ready for another make-out session. Arielle, who had felt blown off all day, was beginning to feel used and accusingly asked Jeb if he just came to see her because he just wanted to hook up. He took that comment as an attack on his character and reminded Arielle he had come all the way to see her and had paid for their entire weekend together. The situation spiraled downhill from there. Not having anywhere to go, Jeb resorted to zoning out by playing *Words with Friends* on his phone, and Arielle spent the night crying in the bathroom. The next morning Jeb drove home, and that was the end of their relationship.

Spending an extended amount of time together can be fatal in the beginning. If you hardly know someone and that person doesn't really know you, miscommunications can easily be made and expectations can be unfulfilled. Just because you are dating someone long distance doesn't exempt you from certain dating rules. You must still end your dates at the *Height of Impulse*. Suggest that the guy get a hotel (you can even do the research for him) or, if you must, only plan for him to stay with you for a night. Perhaps he has other friends he can visit in the area? It may be a long way for him to travel just to see you for a short period of time, but you are worth it. If you want him in it for the long haul, you can't cut corners here. Although you may be fantasizing about a romantic weekend together, the reality is that too much time together too soon is never a good thing. Dating is a marathon, not a sprint. You need to pace yourself no matter what the circumstances.

Was It Something I Said?

What Should I Talk about on Dates?

~~~~~~

Dear Jess,

I never know what to talk about on dates. I usually just let the guy start the conversation and see where that leads us. The only thing is that I get scared that we will get stuck for topics and I'll seem boring! How can I calm my nerves, and should I come prepared with my own questions?

Glad you brought this up! The first date is important, and naturally you want it to go as well as possible. The reason that you are so nervous on your dates is because you are allowing the guy to control the conversation. A great way to quell those nerves and keep the table talk spicy is to ask your date questions about himself! Everyone loves talking about his or her own beliefs and interests, so by preparing some standard questions of your own, you will not only calm your first date jitters, but you will also have your guy thinking you are the best conversationalist on the planet! On top of that, asking good questions will also enable you to get to know this guy much quicker and be able to gauge if he is, in fact, the right person for you.

Other books may have told you to avoid discussions involving sensitive subjects such as politics and religion, warning that you may end up in a heated debate, but I can't think of a better way to start that fire between you! Whether you agree or disagree, topics such as these tell you a lot about the other person and provide interesting table talk. Remember, the key to a great first date is having fun. If you stick to boring, neutral subjects like your jobs and the news, the conversation won't be very stimulating. Ask him about his religion (if he has one). Does he go to church? Does he believe in God? Who did he rally behind in the last election? Does he consider himself socially liberal or conservative?

But those two topics are not the only fodder for get-to-know-you talk; ask about his goals, passions, or his philosophy on life. A good way to begin is by putting a small spin on everyday questions. Instead of asking where he lives or what he does for a living, ask *why* instead. Why did he choose to live in this area? Or why did he decide to go into that profession? "Why" makes even the most mundane questions more interesting, and you will find out more about his motivation and thought process this way. You will also see that men are incredibly fond of women that make them think! As long as you pepper in some lighter questions, such as *where have you traveled recently* and *what's your favorite movie,* to balance the deeper ones, you will be able to really get to know this man without having the conversation sound like an interview.

Can I Ask about His Past Relationships?

Dear Jess,

I really want to know about his past relationships. Is that okay to ask on a first date? Or will that freak him out?

Although it used to be considered taboo, asking about the ex is now not only permitted, it's necessary. Who he dated, what he liked about her, and why they broke up will tell you about the kind of woman he is attracted to and what his thoughts are on relationships. *Asking now, when you are in a position of strength and when he is clearly chasing you, is the best time to do it.*

Was It Something I Said?

Be mindful of your delivery, however. You don't want to bring up his ex out of the blue. Rather, you want to build toward the question by guiding the conversation in that direction. In the same way an attorney would lead a witness, you want to lead your date to the topic of his ex. Here is an example of how to do that:

You: How long have you been on Match.com?
Your Date: I just got on a month ago actually.
You: Oh, what made you want to try it?
Your Date: I broke up with someone a few months ago and
thought this would be a good way to get back out there.
You: How long did you date your ex before it ended?
Your Date: For two years.
You: Wow, that's a long time. What happened?

By being a great listener, you will find cues in his commentary that will allow you to segue into his past. If he doesn't offer much for you to work with, you can start with a relatively benign relationship question and build from there. For example, you can ask your date, "What is the most unusual way you've ever met someone?" or "How long was your longest relationship?" If you guide the conversation with leading questions, the flow will be much more natural and less investigative. Then, when the timing feels right, you can ask more in-depth questions about his former flames. Don't worry about getting too personal. You are dating this man. Getting personal is required if you are going to have a healthy relationship. If you don't inquire about his past, how will you ever truly get to know him?

Not asking these questions can adversely stifle the progress of your relationships as well, and that is exactly what happened to my client Cameron. She was extremely guarded when it came to personal topics. She felt she had to go on several dates with a man before she could bring up prior relationships and other personal information. But after three or four dates of discussing only things like travel and sports, men became bored and eventually stopped calling her. They felt they weren't getting to know Cameron and didn't feel a connection to her. One man even admitted that he didn't feel comfortable making a move to kiss her because she seemed so closed off.

Remember, the purpose of dating is to get to know each other and hopefully develop a bond between you that leads to a relationship. That is something you can't do if you stay on only neutral territory. You may feel overwhelmed with fear just thinking about posing these questions, but I assure you that this isn't a danger zone. You aren't going to scare men off or say anything offensive. Understand that men have a much thicker skin than you might realize, and they take their cues from you on a first date. If you don't dig into their lives, they won't feel comfortable digging into yours.

There is only one thing to be cautious of when talking about exes, however, and that is that you do not chatter on and on about yours. If he does ask about your past, *stick to the facts.* You can tell him how long you dated and why you broke up, but remain unemotional. If you start cursing your ex's name or crying over how much he hurt you, your date will be asking for the check before you've even finished your appetizer.

Was It Something I Said?

How Much Should I Reveal about Myself on a Date?

Dear Jess,

I am never quite sure how much to reveal about myself on a date. I have heard it's best to be "mysterious," but I am not sure what that means or how to even do that. Also, I feel like I am not really that interesting to begin with! What's the best way to tell a guy about yourself so that he likes what he hears and wants to keep seeing you?

Here is some news that may put your fears to rest. The guy you are dating already thinks you are interesting! Otherwise he would have never asked you out. Even if you see yourself as ordinary, he doesn't. To him you are new and exciting. You are fun and fresh. You are impressive, engaging, and captivating, and that is why you are out on a date. As you get to know each other, you can either support his theory on you, or you can defy it. The choice is yours. If you've been set up on a blind date, just remember that, at the very least, someone you both know thinks you are a good fit and most likely his type.

Being mysterious does not mean being tight-lipped about yourself and evading personal questions, as we've previously discussed. A man who is truly interested in you will want to know all about you, and that is a good thing, but there is a difference between letting a man get to know you and telling him all your deepest secrets and insecurities. Telling him stories about your family or your adolescent years is one thing; revealing you had an eating disorder in high school or are still working through your abandonment issues is quite another. No man will want to date you if you seem like an emotional wreck. Therefore, venting about anyone who hurt you, deceived you, or in any other way scarred you in your life is a taboo topic. If you find yourself verbal vomiting all your fears and past disappointments on your dates, it may be time to put meeting guys on hold until you resolve those issues within yourself.

If you are footloose and emotionally baggage-free of your past, talking about your life should not be a problem. It's not so much *what* you say about yourself, but how you say it. You should never embellish or fabricate information to sound more interesting. You simply want to tell the story of you in the most colorful way possible.

Your life isn't boring, but it will sound boring if you present it as so. The key is to tell mini stories about yourself as opposed to giving one-worded general statements. Talk in specifics! Here are some examples:

He asks: What do you do for a living?
Boring answer: I'm a nurse.
Better answer: I got my nursing degree from Georgetown University last year and now I'm working at the hospital in the NICU, which is the intensive care unit for babies.
He asks: What do you like doing on the weekends?
Boring Answer: I like to eat out, exercise, and hang out with friends and family.
Better Answer: I love to try new restaurants. I had Indian food for the first time last week, and it was amazing! I am training for a 10k right now, so that takes up a lot of my free time, and I am really close with my sister so I often spend time with her on the weekends.

If you love your life and show excitement about it, your date will mirror your enthusiasm. Most women stumble on the self-talk because they don't take any time to sit down, think, and prepare their story. Before you start dating, write down all the interesting aspects of your life. Things you've done, places you've been, achievements you've made or are working toward. If you have trouble, ask your friends and family what they find most interesting about you. Then, take those golden nuggets and weave them into a fun and interesting story—your story!

Just be careful not to offer up your personal gold unprompted. If you tell a man that you're a black diamond skier, two-time pageant winner, and world-class speed-reader, and all he asked was what you like to drink, you will seem boastful and arrogant. Wait for the right time to tell him the great things that make you, you— when he asks! Remember to use *The K.I.S.S Principle* so you don't monopolize the conversation, and always reciprocate his curiosity by asking him questions, too.

One thing to avoid when it comes to the self-talk: anything negative! Self-deprecation is funny at times, but someone that doesn't know you well can misunderstand it. Ask yourself, *what does this guy need or want to know about me?* Your passions in life? Yes. Your family? Yes. Your opinions, interests, and life philosophies? Yes, yes, and yes. Your bossy, draining coworker? No. The drama with your mom or sister? No. You want to avoid all bitching, complaining, and bad-mouthing. Even if this guy seems understanding, he will walk away from the date feeling sucked dry. You may feel good when you get out all of your pent-up frustrations, but your date will feel exhausted.

Being mysterious is essentially a term meant to remind you not to reveal your feelings about him too soon. You don't have to be vague on the other aspects of your life, just on your feelings about him. Some women fall in love very quickly and their words and actions make that obvious. You do want him to think you enjoy his company, but you do not want him to think you are ready to reserve a church and pick out china patterns. If you are a hopeless romantic and often don your heart on your sleeve, use the *Mirror Theory* once again to make sure you aren't coming on too strong.

Can I Ask Him His Thoughts on Marriage?

Dear Jess,

Can I ask him about marriage? How do I bring that up? It's really important to me to date a guy who wants to get married someday.

Again, it's all in the delivery! If you flat out ask a man on a first date, "Do you think you want to get married in five years?" he may get the impression you are on a mission to marry. However, if you build toward the question and ask in a non-confrontational way, you will be able to have an open conversation about his feelings. Here is a way to build up to asking about marriage:

You: Tell me about your parents. Are they still together?
Your Date: Actually, yes, they are. They've been married for thirty years.
You: That's amazing. What do you think their secret is?
Your Date: I think they love each other, but they also value family above all else. They have been really inspiring to me.

You: Is that how you feel, too? Family above all else?

Your Date: Yes, I do with my family now, and I will when I
    have my own.

In the beginning, try to avoid using the word "marriage" and
instead use "family." It's less likely to set off any alarm bells in his
head. Keep in mind that the goal is to figure out what kind of man
is sitting across from you. You want to know if he's a good fit for
you, but you also want to know if he's got "relationship qualities." If
he is able to talk about relationships, family, and marriage openly,
there is a good chance he is looking for all those things. On the flip
side, if he complains about his friends getting married or tells you
that kids just aren't his thing, take heed. You may learn this is not
a man who wants the same things you do. The marriage question
is more precarious than asking about his ex, so if you can't find
a good opening for it, it is best to leave it for another time. If you
have been dating someone consistently and you want him to know
that you are looking for a commitment, turn to page 179, *How Do I
Tell Him I'm Looking for a Relationship without Freaking Him Out?* There
is a big difference between asking a man his general thoughts on
family and telling him that you are interested in dating only a man
who's intent on marrying. The former can be discussed on the first
few dates; the latter must be timed appropriately.

Should I Tell Him I'm Dating Other Men?

Dear Jess,

   I went on a great first date last night! There was only one
thing that threw me off. At the end of the night he asked if I was

seeing anyone else. I do have a small funnel going, but I wasn't sure if telling him I was dating other guys would scare him off. What should I have said?

If you are on a first, second, or even third date, it's perfectly fine that you are dating other people. At this point, you should be *Filling Your Funnel* with lots of guys so that you don't put too much stock into one. If you haven't read *You Lost Him at Hello* and aren't familiar with the concept of *Filling Your Funnel,* please allow me to elaborate.

When you meet someone you are interested in, there is a tendency to immediately stop looking for anyone else. However, during the first few weeks of getting to know each other, it's a bad idea to assume any date will lead to lasting commitment. What if you realize he has a bad temper? Or he thinks you spend too much money on shoes? (Gasp!) If he's the only guy you've been seeing, once it ends, you have to start again from scratch. But, if you fill your funnel and get to know multiple men at the same time, as one drops off, you still have others who could potentially result in a relationship. Many go into the funnel, with the hopes that one will come out! *Filling Your Funnel* not only saves you from going back to square one, it also prevents you from putting too much effort into one person right away.

The whole concept of the funnel is to help keep you emotionally grounded. Often when you are seeing only one person, you can get overly excited at the prospect of a relationship. You may start daydreaming about your future together, thus creating grandiose expectations after only a few dinner dates. This typically makes you look overeager. Therefore, it's smart to keep your options open and continue to prospect until he asks you to be exclusive.

Was It Something I Said?

The best way to answer any awkward probing like this is to use *The K.I.S.S. Principle* once again. Never dive into a long explanation about how long you've been seeing other men or what the situation is with each of them. When he asks if you are seeing anyone, just tell him, "Not exclusively." That is all you need to say. Although you may feel the need to explain more, don't. In instances like this, the shorter and simpler the better. You don't want to sound like you are bragging, and you don't want to mistakenly divulge something that may turn him off. *K.I.S.S.* the answer, and then you can turn the question around on him and ask, "How about you?"

How Long Should I Date Multiple People—And What about Sex?

Dear Jess,

But I am afraid "filling my funnel" may backfire on me. How long am I allowed to date multiple people?

It's true that the funnel can backfire if you aren't careful. A client of mine was dating a guy who seemed to talk constantly about the other women he was seeing. At times it seemed as if he was bragging about his ability to attract girls. This brings me to rule number one of funnel dating: *The first rule of the funnel is that you don't talk about the funnel.* Some people think it makes them look cool and instigates some sort of *Jones effect** within the people they are dating. I've coached men and women who have boasted about their funnel on dates in hopes that it will incite a bit of competition and

---

* Jones effect is the notion that most people want what other people have.

fuel desire. But instead it leads to annoyance. Your date doesn't want to hear about the other guys you have been seeing, just as you don't want to hear about the women in his life. It's a delicate subject that has to be handled with care. You aren't doing anything wrong by using a funnel; in fact, you are practicing smart dating, but you should be careful not to boast, brag, or hurt any feelings. If you have been dating someone for a month or two, things have been going well, and if your guy asks if you've been seeing other people, be honest and tell him, "I have been out on other dates, but I haven't found a connection like this with anyone else."

This brings me to the second rule of the funnel. *Do not sleep with anyone in your funnel.* I had a client who had three guys in her funnel, and she slept with whomever was giving her the most attention. Besides risking your physical and mental health, this is a good way to get a bad reputation and ruin your chances for a solid relationship. The use of the funnel is to get to know lots of people and see who you like. It is not a hall pass for casual sex.

As long as you adhere to these two principles, you don't have to worry about the funnel coming back to haunt you. As far as how long you should be dating multiple people, the key is to remember that the funnel is a temporary holding pattern. It's meant to let you get to know men while eliminating the pressure of having to have the relationship work out. Once you know a man is definitely not right for you, you should let him go. This should take only four to eight weeks at most. If the relationship does not progress in that time period, it's time to move on. Do not keep multiple guys in your funnel and attempt to have relationships with all of them. Keeping someone in your funnel, hoping to eventually wear them down into wanting a commitment, is a bad idea. Some men are happy being a long-term casual "hookup" and are perfectly content being one of many. Do not let this happen, because it will severely inhibit your chances of finding that right person for you.

What Should I Say When He Asks Why I'm Not Married?

Dear Jess,

What do I say if a guy asks why I don't have a boyfriend, or worse, why I'm not married yet? I never know what to say, and I feel like a loser when this comes up.

While this question may cause you panic or peevishness, there is a way to handle it with poise and grace. You can keep your response light and flirty, and say, "I guess we both lucked out, being single at the same time." (After all, if you are dating him, he's not with anyone either!) Or you can answer him more seriously. If you do want to address your single status head on, don't discredit your previous relationships. Even though they didn't work out or lead to marriage, they were significant to you. Here is an example of what you can say: "I was involved with someone for (x number of) years, and while it was serious, I didn't see it working out for the long term. We finally ended, and although it was hard, it was the right thing to do."

Just because you never married or don't currently have a significant other doesn't mean you haven't been fortunate in your love life. A relationship does not have to be permanent to be worthwhile or successful. The worst thing you can do here is over-explain why all your past relationships didn't work out or place blame on the male population in general. You are a smart, beautiful woman who isn't in a rush to get married. There is nothing about that that says "loser" to me.

It's up to you how much information you want to share with regard to this question. The only important thing to remember is to stick to the facts once again and remain unemotional.

Should I Ask Him Why He's Still Single?

Dear Jess,

When I ask most guys why they are still single, they just tell me they haven't met the right person. Should I accept that answer or dig further?

If the man you are asking is twenty-seven, you could accept that answer, although I am always going to advise digging until you get to the root of things. If he's thirty-seven, I would definitely dig further. Some men genuinely have a hard time meeting women they like, but others date quite frequently and still maintain they haven't found the one. You need to figure out if he really hasn't found the right person, or if he himself hasn't realized out how to *be* the right person. Very few men are going to come out and tell you that they are the source of their own problem. If he has dated a number of women throughout the years and seems to always be in a relationship but unable to take that last big step, then he may think he's not to blame, but the proof is in his track record. Jump to page 172, *How Do I Figure Out If He Will Want a Relationship?* to learn how to ask about that.

Was It Something I Said?

What Should I Do When the Check Arrives?

Dear Jess,

I'm always uncomfortable at the end of a dinner date. When the bill comes, I am not sure how to handle payment. Do I offer to pay my half? Or do I let the guy pick up the whole thing?

When the waiter drops the tab on your table, there is no need to second-guess what you should do. If you are on a first date, he pays. (For all you gay men out there: Whoever did the asking pays.) You can reach for your wallet, but if he takes your money, he can also take a hike. He's not genuinely interested and you should move on. On the second or third date, you should do "the reach" or ask if you can pick up the tip, but if he's a gentleman, he still won't let you do more than offer. The only thing I recommend against doing is pretending you don't notice the check or make this the time to use the bathroom. It's extremely presumptuous, and the guy will take note of it. By the third or fourth date, it's a good idea to start reciprocating. Pay for the pre-dinner drinks at the bar or take him out for coffee or ice cream. Men do worry about being used for "dinner-only" dating, so it's imperative you reciprocate his generosity. And as I mentioned before, remember to always show gratitude at the end of your dates by saying a sincere "thank you."

One of my clients refuses to offer to pay regardless of how long she is seeing someone. She calls herself "traditional" and believes it is the man's job to pick up the tab, even though she herself makes a sizable income. She is still single at forty and refuses to face the fact that times have changed. Men date her for a few months and usually break things off in a very bitter way.

How and When Should I Talk about Money?

Once you are in a full-blown relationship, you need to have a serious discussion about money. If you earn the same living as he does, it is only fair as you continue your relationship to pay for half of the dating expenses. However, if you earn less, you will have to talk about what you can contribute. These days, men and women make comparable wages, so it really isn't fair to make the man always buy dinner just for tradition's sake. Smart men won't stand for it nowadays, and many will dump you if they feel unappreciated and taken advantage of. Here are some suggestions for broaching the subject of money and expenses:

1. Tell him how you feel about your situation.

Start off with, "I'm embarrassed to have to talk about this," or "I hate to bring this up with you but . . ." He will appreciate that even though this is a difficult conversation for you to have, you are doing the right thing by discussing it with him.

2. Suggest cutting back on spending.

He will take this as a sign of you being responsible as well as not presuming he will gladly take over as your sugar daddy.

3. Ask him how he wants to handle expenses moving forward.

Maybe you come to an agreement right on the spot. For example, he pays for dinners, and you pay for lunches. Or perhaps it's something you will have to discuss as your financial situation changes over time. Whatever the case, be sure to remain sensitive to his generosity and be gracious whenever he foots the bill.

My client Mona had been dating Richard for three months when she had the money conversation with him. Mona makes about half the income Richard does, but she insisted on paying for half their expenditures. Then one day Mona realized that she could not afford to continue spending money in the same manner. She decided to sit down with Richard and have a conversation about what she could contribute. Here is what she said:

> This is very embarrassing for me, but I have to talk about my financial situation with you. I love going out to dinner and to the movies with you; however, I really need to cut back on spending money. Perhaps we can cook more at home or rent a movie instead of going to one?

Once Richard heard this, he told Mona not to worry, and to pay only when she felt she could afford it.

The worst way to handle a situation like this is to stop paying your half and not talk about it with the guy you are dating. Even if it's embarrassing or uncomfortable for you, it is better to communicate your position so he understands your behavior. Otherwise, he may think you are just using him for extracurricular activities.

If, on the other hand, you are in a relationship with someone who makes less than you, you should have the reverse conversation. A relationship must be balanced to be healthy and successful, so if one of you cannot afford to monetarily contribute as much as the other, make sure that the lower earner is putting in a little sweat equity. Maybe the lower earner can't split the expenses, but perhaps he or she can do more of the cooking, organizing, or errand running to make up for it.

If you are dating someone who seems content to let you pay for everything with little concern for giving back to you in any way, consider that a red flag. You may be dealing with someone who has a major flaw in his or her character. To learn more about fatal flaws, jump to page 172, *How Do I Figure Out If He Will Want a Relationship?*

Do I Have to Kiss Him on a First Date?

Dear Jess,

I have a dilemma! I don't like kissing on a first date. I feel like I need to know the guy better first, but I am worried that if I don't let him kiss me, he will think I don't like him and not ask me out again. How can I end the date without kissing but still let him know I'm interested?

You don't have to kiss a guy to let him know you're keen on him. In fact, holding off on the kiss can build anticipation and create even more excitement between you. There are other ways to tell a man you like him and would like to see him again. Here are a few suggestions:

1. Use his name frequently.

It's often referred to as the most beautiful sound in the world. When someone you like says your name, it can send tingles up your spine. Use his name several times throughout the night to let him know you like him and feel connected to him. It will leave him with little doubt that you are enjoying his presence.

Was It Something I Said?

2. Compliment him.

We love to get them, but we don't often return the favor. Make him feel special by complimenting him on something you genuinely like about him—his humor, his quick wit, or even his cute smile. Most men don't get nearly enough compliments, so he will most certainly appreciate the flattery.

3. Go in for the kiss (on the cheek).

Just because you don't want to go full lip-to-lip doesn't mean you can't kiss him somewhere else. Instead of awkwardly waiting for him to initiate the kiss that you are trying to avoid, take control and plant a sweet one right on his cheek. Linger there for a minute so he knows you liked doing it.

You don't have to do anything physical to let a man know you like him. You can convey just as much interest holding his hand and smiling as you can with a kiss or a passionate make-out session. If he leans in or asks if he can kiss you and you aren't ready, simply give him a side peck on the corner of his mouth and tell him that you are shy and like to save real kisses for when you know someone a bit better. Or if you are a little bolder you can say, "I'd love to kiss you right now, but the timing is not yet right for me." Then give him a sly smile and say, "But when the time does come, watch out!"

If you feel like your guy may be getting bored because you have not made out or had sex with him yet, jump to page 75, *Will He Lose Interest If I Don't Sleep with Him?*

Should I Say Yes to a Date on Short Notice?

Dear Jess,

I've noticed that most guys don't like planning ahead. Can I say yes to a short-notice date? How do I get a man to make advance plans?

Books like *The Rules* would firmly scold you if you ever accepted a date without at least three days' notice. But what if you are sitting around Saturday morning with no plans for the night and your new love interest calls to say he has an extra ticket to the baseball game? It's fine to accept a last-minute date as long as *it's few and far between.* Just don't make a habit of always being available at a moment's notice. If you worry you may be sending him the wrong message by saying yes right away, tell him you'd love to go but ask if you can call him back in an hour after you've checked your schedule. This way you can at least make him wait a bit for your answer, and you won't agonize as much about compromising your rules.

If a guy always asks you out at the last minute, then you're going to have to stop saying yes. The only way to break him of his last-minute pattern is to turn the date down when he calls and suggest another time in the future. Try saying this: "Oh, I'd love to see you, but I already have plans tonight. I wish you had called me earlier. Can we do another night?" If he says yes and plans for another night, great. Your problem is solved. If he says he will call you another time and then proceeds to pull another short one on you, repeat the same response as before. Eventually he will get the hint that if he wants to see you, he has to plan ahead. If he never learns and you never go out with him, don't worry. His lack of planning has nothing to do with how much he likes you. This is another clue into a man's character, and you just may have saved yourself from a big headache.

Julie, a long-standing client of mine, met a "last-minute guy" at a Fourth of July party. Steve stuck to her like glue the entire evening and asked for her number well before she left with her friends. Around six the next evening, he texted her and asked her out to dinner for that night. She politely declined and told him she already had plans. She encouraged him to ask her again in the next couple of days, though. The weekend came, and Friday afternoon Steve texted to ask her out for that night again. Julie politely declined once more but reinforced she would love to see him and simply needed more notice. This went on for three months! It wasn't that Steve didn't figure out he needed to ask earlier; he just didn't want to plan ahead. Men who call only on short notice are typically not looking for a real relationship. They don't like making plans ahead of time because they don't like committing until the very last minute. They worry something better will come along, so they keep their calendars wide open. Then, when it becomes apparent that nothing else is going on, they pick up the phone and make their plans. There is nothing you can do to change this behavior. This is simply how some men think.

Three years later, Julie is happily married and Steve is still very single.

If a man is constantly waiting until the eleventh hour to call you, don't waste too much time on him. Realize that his actions are telling you about his emotions—and his emotions are the non-committal type. However, in most relationships, there does come a point after a few months when it becomes assumed that you will be spending certain nights or weekends together, and the firm planning on the guy's part begins to dwindle. This is normal. To learn more about how to handle the transition from planned to presumed dates, jump to page 197, *How Can I Get Him to Make Plans in Advance?*

Can I Plan a Date?

Dear Jess,

I've been dating someone for a few weeks, and so far he has planned all of our dates. There is a concert at the Kennedy Center next month and I really want to go with him. Is it okay for me to plan a date at this point?

It is fine to take initiative and plan a date yourself as long as your new guy has been consistent in calling and seeing you, and there is little doubt that the two of you are headed to relationship town. If, however, you just want to bait him by waving tickets in his face because he's been missing in action or you want him to like you more, I would rethink your strategy. How mad will you be if he accepts your concert tickets but rejects the idea of being with you? If things have not been going well thus far, it's better to take someone whom you know you will have a relationship with after the curtain call.

To prevent wasting tickets on the wrong person, wait until your guy calls *you* for a date, and then offer the concert to him as a suggestion. If he says he'd like to take you to a movie, tell him that you have tickets to a show and would love for him to be your date. If he's been nothing but a gentleman thus far, you could contact him out of the blue and ask him out unprompted, but you are playing it safer if you just wait for him to reach out first.

If the reason you want to plan a date is because his suggestions just aren't that interesting, you should at least oblige his proposed plans the first few times around. You don't want to insult his ideas or seem high maintenance by continuously altering his dates. After you have been out four or five times, however, you can start recommending things you like doing. If he proposes bowling and you'd prefer to go dancing, you can certainly make that suggestion. Most men feel pressure to plot out a perfect night and will often welcome your ideas. It's a good strategy to say yes to his date before changing the plan, though. Here are some ways to approach doing this:

> *He says:* You want to get dinner at the Mexican place
>   tomorrow night?
> *You say:* Sure, that sounds great. I was just reading about an
>   art exhibit that's going on downtown right now. Would
>   you want to do something like that and grab dinner
>   nearby? I think there is a good Mexican place in close
>   proximity.

Be careful that you don't suggest something out of his typical price range without offering to help pay. If he usually takes you to dinner and a movie and you suggest a night at the opera, he may not be financially equipped for it. You could unintentionally hurt his feelings by alluding to the fact you are looking for more lavish dates than the ones he's been planning.

Can I Ask Him Out?

Dear Jess,

I think my situation is a little different and wanted to get your take. I'm in the military, and I just finished up a tour where I met a guy that really caught my interest! It would not have been possible to go on a date before, but now that we've both returned home, I would really like to ask him out. We are Facebook friends, so should I send him a little note asking him to dinner?

Good question! And one I get quite often. Not because more women are enlisting in the armed forces, but because, like you, many people feel that their situation is different from everyone else's. But it doesn't matter if you are back from a tour of duty or back from the future; my answer will be the same in any odd circumstance. Do not impulsively ask any man on a date out of the blue. You will be setting yourself up for probable, if not certain, rejection.

When I was in sales, I was taught a great deal about cultivating relationships, and trying to close a customer without first building a rapport was considered salesman suicide. You have to feel out your client first, much like you need to feel out this guy to sense if he's interested. What if he has a girlfriend? Or is just getting over a breakup? You may think he's single judging from his Facebook status, but he could have a number of things going on in his love life that you are not aware of. To save yourself from potentially being shot down, first shoot him an e-mail, ask how he's been doing, and get a dialogue going. Look for *Buying Signs*. Did he write back immediately? Ask you questions about your personal life? Make a reference about getting together to catch up? If he likes you, you may find that you don't need to be the one asking for the date. He may beat you to the punch. If he doesn't ever mention getting together, then you have to accept the fact that he may not be interested. Even though you are really crushing on him, you have to understand that he may have other things going on in his life. Don't get overly confident and make a rash move. Test the waters before jumping in headfirst. Sometimes the timing is just off, so it's better not to force something simply because you want it right now.

As I stated earlier, if a man asks you out, he is already interested in you. You accepted, so he knows you are interested, too. The next step is not to wrangle him into a commitment as soon as possible; it's for you to figure out if he is a good guy and if you two are compatible. However, if you are consumed with worry and uncertainty about his feelings or about what the future holds for you as a couple, two things will happen: One, you won't get to know the real him because your judgment will be clouded by your own self-doubt; two, he will sense this doubt and you will become less attractive to him. Fight your fears and keep your head in the right mental state by remembering a few key facts about dating. First, acknowledge that one and *only one* guy will ultimately work out for you in the long run. Every other relationship will end. This may seem discouraging, but if you go into dates expecting all of them to amount to a relationship, you are setting yourself up for disappointment and failure. Understand that you are only looking for that one special person and everyone else is just practice. Second, do not think beyond the date you are on. Daydreaming about your future with a man instead of getting to know him in the here and now will shift your focus from evaluating your compatibility to uselessly worrying about yourself. Stay present on each date and do not think any further than the kiss goodnight.

Chapter Three

HOOKING UP

Leslie had been seeing Nicholas for almost two months when he suddenly disappeared. He had gone out of town on a business trip and told her he would be back in a few days. Over a week later, she had not heard from him, and she was starting to panic.

"I think I did something wrong," she told me as she sat on my couch one afternoon. "I think I may have pushed him away by not being affectionate enough."

"Why do you think that?" I asked.

Leslie chewed on her nails. "Because he is always making remarks about how turned on he is with me. But I never let it get out of hand. Whenever he tried to go further physically, I stopped him."

"Is that a bad thing?" I questioned. "You've only been dating for a couple of months."

Leslie stood up abruptly. It was obvious she was frustrated and antsy.

"Most people don't wait that long anymore though. I don't think he's used to it and I'm afraid he's just giving up on me. I don't even know why I'm holding out. Things have been going so well. He's a great guy and all the signs point to this being a relationship, don't they?" she asked.

I thought carefully about my answer.

"Things have been going well, but there are still a lot of unknown factors at play. We don't know if he's dating other people. We don't know if he's ready for a serious commitment. And we definitely don't know why he hasn't called you since last Saturday," I pointed out. "I don't think lack of sex drove him away. I think something else is going on and it's good that you have been taking this slowly."

Although I tried to reason with her, Leslie didn't seem to agree. When our session ended she gathered her things in a daze and headed out the door.

Three days later she called me with a complete change in attitude.

"He called!" she screamed into the phone. "Everything is fine!"

I was relieved, although still a bit cynical. "I'm so glad you've heard from him. Tell me what happened exactly."

"He called and was acting as if nothing was wrong. He said he missed me and couldn't wait to see me. We are going out tonight," Leslie said.

Immediately my play-dar went off.

"Leslie, I am really glad that he called you. It's obvious he hasn't lost his interest, but I am still leery as to why he went out of town and didn't make any effort to contact you. This is a complete change of behavior for him."

Leslie brushed me off.

"It's fine, Jess. He said he was thinking about me while he was gone, but he was just so busy."

I could tell by her tone that all was forgiven. Then I thought about our last conversation.

"Leslie, are you planning to have sex with him tonight?"

She busted out laughing. "How do you know me so well?" she replied.

"Do you really think that's a good idea? Don't you think it makes sense to wait and make sure this little bump in the road was a fluke and not an indication of what's to come?" I asked her.

But it was obvious my warning was falling on deaf ears.

"Everything is fine, and I know why you're saying that, but there's no way it's not going to happen, Jess. We haven't seen each other in a week and a half. I know that tonight is the night."

"Of course this is your life and your relationship, so you can do anything you want. I just have to say that I don't think it's a good idea right now," I told her.

"I understand, Jess. Thanks for being concerned, but it's definitely going to happen tonight." She laughed. "I know I won't be able to resist."

Leslie hung up the phone after that, and I sat back and crossed my fingers for her.

Just twenty-four hours later, Leslie called me again. This time she was crying hysterically. For the most part, things went according to her plan. Nicholas had picked her up the night before and taken her out to dinner. Afterwards they stopped by a party thrown by Leslie's cousin. At that point he was, as she put it, all over her. Nicholas never left her side, kissed her many times throughout the night, and even told her cousin that he was her new boyfriend. Leslie was not only feeling comfortable, she was on cloud nine. She took Nicholas back to her place, where they proceeded to have sex twice that night and once in the morning.

Around 9:00 a.m. the next day, Leslie got out of bed and put on some coffee. She was late for work, but as long as Nicholas wasn't in a rush, she didn't care. She waited for the coffee to finish brewing, poured it into two big mugs, and headed back to her bedroom. She found Nicholas just where she had left him in bed, except now he was on the phone.

"That sounds great. I will book as soon as I get home," he said. "See you tomorrow."

Leslie stood in her doorway confused.

"What's going on? Are you going somewhere tomorrow?" she asked.

Nicholas hopped out of bed and put on his pants. "No, I'm going somewhere today. To Palm Springs, to hang out and play golf with some buddies. We just decided to take off for the weekend."

Leslie couldn't believe what she was hearing. He had just come back to town after not seeing or talking to her for eight days, and now he was leaving again?

She didn't know what to say except, "Oh. When are you coming back?"

Nicholas took a sip of coffee. "Oh, uh, I think Tuesday? I'm not sure yet. Depends on how much fun we are having. My friend has rented a house for a full week."

Leslie stood there dumbfounded. She watched as Nicholas quickly got dressed and headed out of her bedroom.

"See you when I get back," he said as he gave her a quick kiss on the forehead.

He swung open the door and walked out, letting it close behind him.

"I feel like such a fool!" Leslie cried to me later. "I thought everything was fine. How did you know that this would happen?" she asked me.

"I didn't know what would happen, actually. That's why I advised against sleeping with him. He went from calling every day to disappearing for over a week. That change in pattern was a red flag. If he could vanish before sex, he could vanish just as easily after. I wanted you to wait until you figured him out and knew he would stick around."

"I feel so stupid for not understanding that. You told me, but I didn't listen. Will I ever understand men and be able to figure this out myself?" Leslie asked.

"Yes, of course!" I told her. "You just have to learn a few things that can help you predict a man's behavior. That's actually the easy part. The hard part is not ignoring the prediction once you do."

Studies have shown that men are more likely than women to seek casual sex and are less picky about their partners. So while you may be thinking you have off-the-charts, cosmic chemistry with a guy, he could just be having a good Tuesday night. Of course, not all men are so nonchalant about sex, but there are enough out there to make it a concern.

When you are attracted to someone, hooking up with that person may feel as natural as breathing. However, like most things that feel good, you must be aware of potentially dangerous side effects. In many instances, casual hookups can cause a lot of confusion. Although you may feel like the relationship is headed in the right direction, getting physical too fast can often send you down a dead-end road. Therefore, learning how to handle hookups may be the most important lesson you learn about dating. In the pages to follow, we will discuss several of the most frequently asked hook-up questions, from how to know if someone really likes you or is just interested in fooling around to what to do if your most recent hookup is avoiding you. Is there a good way to tell a guy you aren't ready for sex? And one of the most burning questions of all: Can you turn a one-night stand into a relationship? All these questions and many more are finally answered with detailed advice on how to handle each of them.

The term "hooking up" can really be defined only by the person using it. For some it means making out. For others, it signifies having sex. It is ambiguous slang that is often used to avoid giving details about physically amorous activity. To be clear in regards to the questions below, the term hooking up is meant to be associated with making out. When sex is involved, the word sex will be used.

How Can I Tell If He Likes Me—Or If He's Just Looking for a Hookup?

Dear Jess,

How can I tell if a guy is just looking for a hookup? I've been hooking up with someone for a few weeks, and I'm not sure how to tell if he's truly interested in me or if he just wants someone to fool around with.

If we were playing *Jeopardy!* right now, you would have just hit the daily double. This is the question all single women want answered. How do you determine a man's true interest? There is really only one way to know what a man's intentions are and here it is: To tell if a man genuinely likes you or just wants to sleep with you, you must get to know him *prior* to hooking up with him.

If you meet a guy and hook up with him right away, there is no way to tell if he likes you or just likes fooling around with you. Straight men like making out with women. No surprise there. But there are men out there who will hook up in hopes of having sex with a woman they have no interest in seriously dating. The only way to weed out these types of guys is to date them and get to know them without being physical. Kissing is fine, but even that shouldn't happen until you've been taken on a date first. If you kiss someone before he has taken you out, you are unconsciously telling him *he doesn't have to date you to hook up with you.*

Also, if you hook up with someone before you know him well, your emotions will cloud your judgment of him. Red flags are easier to ignore, and you will be less apt to walk away if you've already been physically intimate. To be objective and truly evaluate a man's character, you have to be clearheaded and unattached emotionally.

However, if you do, in fact, hook up with someone before dating, what then? Now you are confused about his intentions, and not even a tub of Ben & Jerry's will fill that ache in your stomach. You have two choices: Keep hooking up with him because you like him and you don't want to lose what you have, or stop hooking up with him and try to get to know him on an emotional level.

If you stay the course and change nothing, you will eventually end up having sex with this guy. Then you will have put yourself in the very category you were trying to avoid. The only way to even attempt getting something more out of this hookup is to stop hooking up. The next time you hang out with this man, you have to change your usual pattern.

Let's say you and your regular hook-up buddy typically meet up at a bar, have a few drinks, and then go back to his place. You can still keep that routine, as long as you rewrite the ending. When last call approaches, tell your guy that you've had fun hanging out with him, but you've got to be getting home now. He will inevitably look confused and maybe even ask why you aren't coming back to his place. Don't waver. Tell him you want to sleep in your own bed tonight, *but balance this negative with a positive,* and tell him you would like to see him another time. Then, suggest doing something during the daytime. If you have talked before about how you both love to hike, suggest that. Say, "I was thinking about hiking that trail this weekend. Do you want to come along?" If he says he can't, do not panic. He may genuinely be busy or just completely thrown by this change in behavior. Give it some time, but stick to the plan. If you want a relationship, you are going to have to stand up for what you want and not just take whatever opportunity he gives you. Suggesting some sort of fun physical activity such as hiking, biking, or working out is good because it is not as date-like as a movie or dinner, but it's moving in that direction. Hopefully, because you've taken control and limited his access, he will begin to see you as more than just a bed-buddy, and you will be able to get to know him on a deeper level. A good rule to always keep in mind is this: Never let your physical relationship surpass your emotional relationship. Meaning, if you don't feel your hearts and minds are connecting, your bodies shouldn't be either. Staying true to this mantra will help keep you from getting your heart broken.

For advice on how to actually tell him that you don't feel comfortable hooking up until you know each other better, move on to the next question.

Was It Something I Said?

Can I Turn My One-night Stand into a Relationship?

Dear Jess,

I had a one-night stand with a guy friend. Now I think I like him. Is there any way to turn a one-night stand into a relationship?

Typically you cannot have sex and *then* develop a relationship with someone. For this reason it should be avoided at all costs! However, there are those rare instances where a one-night stand actually does turn into something more significant. If you are hoping to have this happen to you, I do have a few tips on how to best make that transpire. The following advice will also help you if you have been dating someone and had sex with him too soon.

1. Pretend you didn't sleep with him.

The biggest mistake you can make is expecting the guy to act differently toward you because you have now had sex. So pretend you didn't, and continue acting as you did before. Don't expect him to call you more often or be more affectionate toward you. That's what happens when someone becomes your boyfriend, and, in this case, you just had sex. Expecting him to suddenly act more interested or connected is the fastest way to frustrate yourself and get angry with him. Believing his feelings will change after sex and being disappointed when they don't leads most girls to pull out their old bag of tricks: ignore him completely, get mad over small things, or make him jealous with other guys. None of these things works, so save yourself the hassle and don't try them. Continue to be yourself. Don't ignore him or act strange;

just expect things to carry on as usual and you might have a shot at a relationship . . . eventually.

2. Don't do it again.

If you want this one-night stand to work out in the long run, you have to compartmentalize this one-time occurrence. It must remain a one-night stand. If you continue to sleep with the guy, your chances for a relationship will deteriorate. A one-night stand can be justified as a mistake made in the heat of passion. A multiple-night stand is called friends with benefits, and it is nearly impossible to turn that into a serious commitment. Just remember: Doing it once is a mistake. Twice is a pattern.

If your one-night stand tries coming on to you again, use *Build–Break–Build* to tell him you like him, but you won't be having sex with him. First, start off with a positive, followed by the inevitable letdown. Then finish with another positive. Here is an example of what you can say:

Build: *I don't regret what happened because I do like you and we have a lot of fun together.*

Break: *It's uncharacteristic of me to have sex with someone so fast (or someone I'm not in a relationship with). I think we got too carried away and need to take a step back.*

Build: *But if you want to keep hanging out and see where this goes, I'd be up for that.*

This will help preserve his respect for you and help you keep yours for yourself. It may also spawn a deeper conversation about his feelings for you. If it doesn't, however, then you have to take his silence as a *Silent No*. Continue to be his friend if you can, and

Was It Something I Said?

if you can't, tell him that the situation has confused you and you need a little space.

If some time has passed and he has not tried to get physical again, and you really want to know where you stand, you can say, "I really want to remain friends with you, but to do that I really need to talk about what happened that night we hooked up."

If he doesn't open up right away, try a few probing questions such as, "Did this happen because you feel there is something between us, or were you [insert a reason that pertains to the situation such as "rebounding from another relationship"]? Remain friendly and open when you ask so he knows you will be accepting of whatever he has to say. Hopefully, you will get some insight into what he's thinking.

In the future, just remember a strong committed relationship should be established before you even consider sex, not after. For more on when to have sex for the first time with someone, jump to page 76, *When Should I First Have Sex with Him?*

I Hooked Up with My Ex. Does He Want Me Back?

Dear Jess,

My ex and I have been broken up for six months. Recently he asked me to get a drink with him, and we ended up hooking up later that night. Does this mean he wants to get back together? He asked me to get together again, but I want to know how he feels. How do I ask him what he wants?

Unfortunately, just because you and your ex took a "strip" down memory lane does not mean you are headed for reconciliation.

Most women assume an old flame wouldn't bother reconnecting without a really good reason. However, that isn't always the case. Right now you need to determine his intentions. Has he realized you were the love of his life, or is he just bored and lonely? There is only one way to know: *Get him to tell you what he wants and then see if he backs it up with his actions.*

Ask him flat out, "What made you want to contact me after all this time?" Take his answer at face value. If he says he was just wondering how you've been, accept that as the truth. Don't assume he's secretly still in love with you but his pride won't let him tell you. A guy can contact an ex-girlfriend for the same reason he contacts his college roommate—nostalgia. The feeling struck him and he acted upon it. Sometimes guys just don't think ahead. Sometimes there is absolutely no deeper meaning behind what they do.

If he isn't gushing over you or being overly affectionate, do not try to hook up with him again in hopes of reigniting his interest. You will only be disappointed when he decides the next day that you were never right for each other.

On the other hand, if he says he really has been missing you, that does indicate that his feelings for you are still there to some extent, but even then you shouldn't assume you are getting back together. Tell your ex you've missed him too and that seeing him was fun. Then tell him to give you a call if he wants to hang out again. Whatever you do, *do not hook up with him again.* It's very common for women to fall back into old patterns with an ex. They may plan to meet for one drink but end up spending the entire weekend at his place. As we discussed before, if you want to know a man's intentions, you have to get to know him prior to hooking up with him. Although you already know your ex, you don't know his intentions this time around. The big danger in hooking up right away is that you won't be able to determine whether he is genuinely looking to rekindle your relationship or if he is simply looking for what I call "ex sex."

What is ex sex? Because it takes a significant amount of time and effort to court a woman, some men revert to digging into their past when they want physical attention. If you've slept with him before, he's already done all of the legwork. He won't have to spend months trying to get you to hook up with him, as he would with someone new. He may not even have to take you on one date! In many circumstances he just has to place a phone call and the rest will take care of itself. Don't fall victim to this plan. Make sure your ex truly does want to get back together. I know it's hard, but you have to treat this relationship as if it were brand new. If he's serious about reconciling, he'll be calling you again. If he tries to hook up with you, use *Build-Break-Build* and let him down gently.

Will He Lose Interest If I Don't Sleep with Him?

Dear Jess,

I've been dating a guy for six weeks and we really get along well. I haven't slept with him yet, though, and I worry that he's losing interest in me. All my friends tell me that six weeks is too long to make a guy wait, and eventually he's just going to move on. Should I sleep with him?

For generations, men have had to wait until marriage to have intercourse. That should tell you that it's not sex that keeps guys interested; otherwise none of us would have been born. *In reality, it's the desire to have sex with someone that keeps men initially interested, not the act of doing it.* If this guy is losing interest in you, something other than you not having sex with him is causing it.

If you have sex because you are afraid that a man will leave you if you don't, the relationship will not work out regardless of whether you sleep with him or not, because you will be compromising yourself for the sake of the guy. And if you think he doesn't know that you are giving in because you are scared to lose him, you could not be more mistaken. Bees and dogs aren't the only things that can smell fear. Single guys can detect it in a single whiff. And just so you know, fear is not sexy.

If a man is not acting interested now, he will be even less interested once you have sex. There is a reason you are hesitant about sleeping with him. Maybe because it's too soon and you don't feel like you know him, or you aren't sure where the relationship is going yet. Listen to that instinct. It is preventing you from making a big mistake. Hopping into bed with him will not secure your relationship, because sex is not a relationship life preserver. Men don't fall in love with women who compromise their values and self-respect, which is just what you would be doing. Instead of thinking about how you might lose him if you don't have sex, think about how he may never call you again if you do.

When Should I First Have Sex with Him?

Here are a few good guidelines on when to have sex. But remember they are just guidelines, and you have to ultimately decide when is the right time for you.

1. Be certain of where your relationships stands before becoming physically intimate.

Sleeping with a guy before you are his wife or girlfriend greatly lessens the chances of attaining that title. If what you want is a serious monogamous relationship, then you must wait to have sex until you've reached that status. *The relationship must always come before sex.* If you think you are in a relationship but haven't had that conversation yet, jump to page 181, *How Do I Bring Up the "Relationship Talk"?*

2. You should at the very least be in a committed, monogamous relationship for several months, if not longer.

A common mentality among singles is to hop into bed as soon as they get the green light on exclusivity. However, just because you are not dating other people doesn't mean you should throw all caution (and clothing) to the wind. You still have to figure out if you are good together as a couple, and sex can often cloud your judgment on that. It also makes leaving a bad relationship more difficult. Make sure you date exclusively for some time to discern if you're well suited to be together.

3. You should be happy with the relationship just the way it is.

If you are, in any way, disgruntled about the way he acts with you, you should not have sex with him. Sex will not turn your relationship around if it is already heading downhill. If you are unhappy now, you will only be more miserable after you have sex. You should already feel connected, in sync, and close to the man you are dating; that's when having sex makes your bond stronger.

If you know that you are not ready to have sex and are uncertain of how to tell your guy, move to the next question, *How Do I Tell Him I'm Not Ready for Sex?*

How Do I Tell Him I'm Not Ready for Sex?

Dear Jess,

My boyfriend recently told me that sex is very important to him in a relationship and that once we have sex we will be closer. I like him and will eventually want to have sex, but I'm not ready right now. How do I tell him he has to keep waiting? Is there anything I can say that will keep him from moving on to someone who is more willing?

Sex is an important component in a serious, committed relationship, but if you aren't ready, then having sex is only going to make you feel awkward and uncomfortable around him. Kudos to you for standing your ground and not doing the deed!

You want to convey to this man that you are interested in sex; however, it has to be with the right person, at the right time, for it to be good for you. There is a way to tell him that you like sex and still maintain your stance on not doing it with him just yet. You want to agree with him before you ultimately disagree with him, using a method called *Feel–Felt–Found* (*FFF*). Here is how it works: "I know how you *feel* about sex, because I have *felt* the same way. It can be such an amazing experience. But what I've *found* for me is that unless I am really comfortable and secure with the other person, I can't let go and enjoy myself. You would want me to be able to do that, right?"

Was It Something I Said?

FFF allows you to express your understanding for the other person's point of view, create harmony between you both because you are saying you feel the same way, but ultimately communicate you've discovered a new and better way to handle the subject (in this case, sex). *FFF* can be used in many other instances, as you will see throughout the book. You can also add a rhetorical question at the end of your *FFF* statement to emphasize the importance of your stance.

What If I Want to Remain a Virgin until Marriage?

If you want to save yourself for marriage, more power to you! Although casual hookups are prevalent, holding out is just as popular. Studies by the National Center for Health Statistics indicate that virginity among single men and women is increasing. So while it may seem like you are the only one taking the road less traveled, you are definitely not traveling alone. You don't need to disclose your plan to stay chaste until you get to know the guy and decide to enter into a relationship. No sense in telling him on the first few dates. When the time comes to get serious, be honest and tell him you'd like to be in a monogamous relationship, but you won't be crossing certain boundaries until you are married. How will he respond? It depends on the kind of guy he is. If he is just looking for sex and has no intention of hunkering down with you for the long haul, he may fade into the distance pretty quickly. However, if he is a good guy and appreciates the connection he has with you, your virginity will not deter him from pursuing the relationship further; in fact, it will only fuel his desire to be with you.

One of my former male clients started dating a woman who, at twenty-nine, was still a virgin. Although he had previously had sex with other women, he completely respected this woman's values—so much so that he quickly fell in love with her. Even though she told him she could not go further than kissing him, he continued to date her. They were together for a year when, one night on a trip to St. Lucia, he proposed. They have now been married for several years.

Using *Feel–Felt–Found* again, you can tell your boyfriend that you love him, but that you won't be having sex until marriage. Here is what you can say: "I know how you feel about sex, because I've felt the same way. I agree that it can bond two people in love and it's essential for a healthy relationship. However, what I've realized (found) is that I only want to have sex with my husband. So I am going to wait until I'm married."

What is most important here is that you say this with conviction. You should not think of yourself as being weird. You should feel empowered by your own choices, and that should come across as you are talking. Don't cringe and look away when you deliver this message. Look your boyfriend straight in the eye and wear a serious expression on your face. This is something to be proud of, like any other personal choice you've made.

Men are fully capable of having monogamous relationships without sexual intercourse. Do not be afraid of your boyfriend's reaction. Assume he is the good guy you think he is and trust that he will react in a positive way. And remember, men respect women who respect themselves.

How Do I Get My Hookup to Take Me on a Real Date?

Dear Jess,

I'm hooking up and hanging out with a guy I really like and who seems to like me, too. He texts me a lot and is always asking to see me. I can't say we are "dating" though, because he has never taken me on an actual date! We just rotate between hanging out at his place and mine. I can feel myself getting angry and frustrated. Is he just using me? Not that into me? Or is he just lazy and cheap? What can I say to him to get him to take me on a real date?

As you date, you will begin to realize that not all guys are alike. In fact, some of them can be so different it's like dating another species. While some prefer to wine and dine out on the town, others may favor the comfort and privacy of their own home. (This is especially true for college guys or younger men who are just starting out in the workplace.) Do not assume that if he hasn't taken you to dinner that he doesn't like you. Yes, he could be cheap and lazy, but it could also be that he stayed in with all his past girlfriends, so he's doing what feels natural to him.

You should absolutely talk to your guy about this because, as evident from your question, you are becoming increasingly frustrated and will eventually erupt if you don't speak your mind. *But before you unload grievances, you want to figure out how he feels about the way you spend time together.* In Christian Carter's book, *Catch Him, Keep Him,* he advises to "seek to understand before seeking to be understood." Rather than kicking off the conversation with your complaints and frustrations, put the criticism aside and instead ask this man questions to figure out what his expectations are. Here is a good way to start off the conversation:

> *You:* I realized the other day that we stay in most of the time. Do you prefer staying in, rather than going out?
> *Him:* I guess. I'm tired at the end of the day, so I don't feel like doing much. It's nice to just relax on the couch.
> *You:* Is this how you've always felt, or has anything changed recently that has made you like staying in more?
> *Him:* I got a new boss six months ago and he works me to death. I'm also working really hard to save up money to buy my condo, so I prefer staying in than spending money on expensive drinks or dinners out. I figured you felt the same way, don't you?

Sometimes you won't get the last part ("I figured you felt the same way"). If your man is insightful and intuitive, he will pick up on the fact that there is a reason you are having this conversation in the first place. But don't be too hard on him if he doesn't connect the dots. At the very least you understand why you aren't being taken out, and that it has little to do with you. If there were ever a good reason to stay in and save money, buying a house would be it. It shows that your man is thinking ahead and being responsible. After he's told you his side, you are free to express your point of view. Knowing more about his thought process will hopefully keep you from saying anything insensitive or inappropriate. Here is an example of how to best express your point of view on this topic: "I think it's great that you are saving money for a house. I was hoping to try that new Thai restaurant down the street sometime. Would you be open to going out to dinner once next week?"

Was It Something I Said?

Making a small request like this is better received than telling your guy you need to be taken out at least twice a week from now until eternity. Start small and build toward finding a good middle ground. If he pushes back on you and adamantly declares he prefers staying in, then you may have to accept you won't be going out as much as you want, or move on and find a guy that is more your speed. But first try to get your guy to compromise by saying the following. "I'm learning that we are somewhat different in how we like to spend our free time. I really enjoy trying new restaurants and lounges. Is there a good compromise we can come to so that we both get to do the things we like together?"

If, after having your conversation, you feel like the reason your guy doesn't take you out is because he is interested only in hooking up with you, do not ignore those feelings. Tell him you are unhappy with how things are, and, using "I feel" once again, explain that the relationship isn't giving you what you need. If he turns the conversation around on you by calling you high maintenance, it may be time to give the relationship a little break.

This type of scenario where two people have conflicting points of view is very common. It's something you will encounter many times when dating, so remember to ask questions and seek to understand before making complaints or critiques.

Should I Call the Guy I Hooked Up with at a Party?

Dear Jess,

I went to a party with some friends and happened to meet a really cute guy. By the end of the night we were all really drunk.

The guy invited us back to his place, where he and I started hooking up. I kept asking him if he was just doing this because he was drunk, but he reassured me that he really liked me. Now it's been two weeks and I haven't heard from him! Should I call him and find out what happened?

Let's do a quick recap of the situation. You went to a party, met a complete stranger, got drunk, hooked up with him, and now you are wondering why he hasn't called you. Even though you thought you were being careful by asking him his intentions up front, given he had known you only a few hours what was he really supposed to say? "No, I don't like you. I'm totally wasted and I won't even remember your name tomorrow?" He might have been drunk, but he's not stupid.

To answer your question, there really isn't much you can do. He's avoiding you for a reason. If you reach out to him, you probably won't get a good response. Unfortunately, he doesn't see you for the smart, funny, independent woman that you are. He doesn't know that you play piano or graduated with honors. How could he? You spent a few hours drinking with him at a party. All he knows of you at this point is that you like Captain and Coke and wear a purple bra. You've labeled yourself as a hookup from the very start. It's hard to change that first impression.

I know you are dying to redeem yourself and show him how great you really are, but any attempts to get in touch with him now will only make you look desperate. You will be immediately classified as a stage-five clinger for ignoring his obvious sign of disinterest. Unfortunately, the best thing to do here is nothing—except learn from your mistake and not do it again.

Was It Something I Said?

If you have made a bad impression on a guy, but have *not* hooked up with him yet, jump to page 97, *How Do I Correct a Bad First Impression?*

What Should I Do If I Hooked Up with a Guy from Work?

Dear Jess,

I know I shouldn't have done this, but I hooked up with a guy at work! I've liked him for a really long time, and at a recent work happy hour we got to talk a lot. At the end of the night we did make out quite a bit. Now he's acting very distant at work, and whenever I see him it's awkward. We had such a great night together; I am really surprised this isn't going anywhere. What happened, and is there anything I can do? What should I say when I see him?

There is a reason that romance in the workplace is often frowned upon. It's awkward for you, for him, and sometimes for others. When you are dating someone you don't work with, he has to put effort into seeing you again. If you work with him, that key element is eliminated. He gets to see you the very next day, whether he wants to or not. Naturally, you shouldn't have kissed him because he hadn't asked you out on a date yet, but at least he wasn't a random guy. This situation isn't as black and white as some others. How you handle yourself and what you say to him are going to depend on the kind of guy you are dealing with.

You said you've known and liked him for a while, so the first thing to do is assess what kind of person he is. How you deal with a guy who is quiet and reserved will be a lot different from how you behave with someone who charms the pants off every girl in the office (figuratively or literally). If he's more on the shy side, send him an e-mail, telling him you had a good time talking to him the other night, and that you hope, above all else, that he doesn't feel uncomfortable around you at work. That's it. *Remember The K.I.S.S. Principle and keep it short and simple.* Make sure you allow enough time for him to talk to you about the situation first. If he has acted funny for only a day or two, you may need to be a bit more patient and give this guy a little more time to come around.

If he's more of the player type, and he flirts with lots of women in the company and is in general a social butterfly, your strategy will be the opposite of that. Make yourself scarce. Don't try to run into him on purpose. In fact, if you can avoid him for a while, that would be best. The reason is, if he's a real lady's man, chances are you aren't the only girl at work who has the hots for him. You may not even be the only one he's hooked up with, so you don't want to lump yourself in with all the other women vying for his attention. You may also have to accept that he may be quite the womanizer and that your brief encounter with him may not have meant as much to him as it did to you. The only way to tell is to back off and see if he comes after you. A charming, confident man won't have any problem going after what he wants. If he does, make sure you take things slow going forward. If you don't know which strategy will work best because you really can't tell what type of guy he is, jump to page 172, *How Do I Figure Out If He Will Want a Relationship?*

Most men don't like to have their love lives on display at work, so no matter what kind of guy he is, you should always be discreet when dealing with office romance. Don't hang around his desk, forward him silly e-mails, or try to time your lunch breaks so that you run into him. Go about your day as usual, and remember to act as if nothing has changed because quite honestly, nothing really has yet. You are still just coworkers, so until you become more than that, stick to your usual work demeanor.

What Should I Do When It's Awkward the Morning after a Hookup?

Dear Jess,

I always feel so awkward the day after I first hook up with someone new. I wake up in the morning and never know what to say or do. Should I suggest breakfast? Should I wait and see what he wants to do? Should I just leave as quickly as possible? Please advise!

When the lights are on and the alcohol's gone, things never seem as hot as they did eight hours ago. If you feel awkward the morning after you've hooked up with a guy, it can mean only one thing: You've hooked up with him too soon. Of course you feel uncomfortable. You just woke up next to a complete stranger. He may dress well and have washboard abs, but the fact remains that he's still a stranger. Seeing him around or going on a few dates with him does not constitute knowing him. What did he say his last name was again? Yes, it's definitely too soon.

But because you are already in the midst of the situation, I will tell you what I recommend. I would advise leaving as soon as possible in the morning. The reason being, if you feel awkward and

Hooking Up

unsure of what to do with yourself, chances are he feels awkward and unsure of what to do with you, too.

Get out of bed, go to the bathroom, and tidy yourself up. When you finish, go over to the bed and gently wake him up. The key here is to act as if you are relaxed, even if you aren't. Tell him good morning and thank him for last night's date again. Then say you have to be somewhere by nine (or whatever time makes sense) and that you have to get going. Lean over, give him a kiss on the cheek (or forehead, in case of morning breath), and then tell him you will show yourself out.

This is the best way to handle the awkwardness of the morning after. What you don't want to do is wait around to see what he will do when he wakes up. Don't sit there like a puppy waiting to be walked and fed. There is no reason to linger around in the morning right now. Once you are in a solid committed relationship, you can lounge around his house drinking espresso and reading the paper. But for now, it's time to get out before he kicks you out.

If you happen to be at your place, tell him you have an early morning obligation. Get up, get dressed, and he will follow suit. You won't have to tell him to leave. As you walk out together you can kiss him on the cheek before heading to your car (and driving once around the block).

This advice applies even if the guy suggests grabbing coffee or breakfast together. It's a good sign he's still interested, but keep in mind the *Height of Impulse.* Simply tell him you would love to, but you'll have to take a rain check. Then give him a big smile and be on your way!

Why Did My Boyfriend Suddenly Become Distant?

Dear Jess,

I met my boyfriend at a party two months ago, and we just recently had sex. It seems like the minute after we did it, he completely changed. He was so attentive before; now he acts hot and cold around me. I thought sex was supposed to bring us closer, and instead he's more distant! How do I change this?

It's hard to say what is going on here without more detailed information about this relationship. You could very possibly be dating a guy who essentially stops trying once he has sex with a woman. However, because you used the word "attentive" to describe his previous behavior, I'm also wondering if your expectations are just a bit too high. There is no doubt that men are on their best behavior in the beginning, and whatever you want, big or small, they will jump through hoops to make it happen. However, you have to realize that you would have a completely lopsided relationship if he catered to you 100 percent of the time. Eventually you should both relax and settle into a partnership where you both do nice things for each other and the word "attentive" should be replaced with other adjectives like "affectionate," "reliable," and "loving." The word "attentive" makes me think of someone waiting on you hand and foot, and that is something a waiter does, not a boyfriend.

On the flip side, "hot and cold" behavior implies that your man goes from one extreme to the other. He's all over you one minute and then seems to want nothing to do with you the next. This definitely does not make for a healthy relationship, but I don't think sex caused him to act this way; rather, it *allowed* him to relax and be himself more. Unfortunately for you, his true self seems to be a rather moody person.

Next time you feel your boyfriend is being cold, ask yourself if he's really acting cold or if you are just expecting a bit too much from him. If you get upset because he doesn't jump to refill your cocktail without asking, or forgets to compliment your new haircut, you may need to re-explore what it means to be in a relationship with someone. However, if he completely ignores you when you are with his friends, or shuts down when you try talking to him about anything serious, you may need to question what you are doing with this guy in the first place. There certainly are men that lose interest after sex, so if he's "hot" when he wants some physical attention but "cold" when you're doing other relationship-type things, he may simply be stringing you along because he wants to keep you as a regular hookup.

Moody selfish behavior should be at the top of your dealbreaker list. If your man directs his unfounded moodiness at you, the best thing to do is completely disengage. Don't coddle him, be affectionate toward him, or attempt to make him happy by doing extra nice things. That is tantamount to giving a three year old an ice-cream cone for throwing a tantrum. Don't reward his negative behavior. Instead, try saying this to him: "You're obviously in a bad mood. I don't want to be around you when you're like this. Give me a call when you're feeling better."

Then get up and leave. If you have tried coaxing him to open up without success and he's being extremely unreasonable, it's time to switch strategies. It's best to use *Mirror Theory* in these circumstances and imitate his mood rather than attempt to change it. If he's acting distant from you, then become distant both mentally and physically from him. Hopefully after a few times, he will realize that if he wants to keep you around, he has to keep his attitude in check. Men often respond better to action, so although your natural instinct is to try to talk it out, if his mood is unwarranted, you have to teach him his behavior is unacceptable.

At its core, the problem with hooking up is that once you do it with someone you begin to expect a certain behavior from that person. You have allowed a guy to get to know you intimately, and so going forward you may assume he will treat you with a certain level of closeness. But most men aren't going to treat you any differently after they hook up with you. Knowing this, you have to be the one to decide if you are satisfied with your relationship beforehand.

Some women are able to have meaningless sex; others become smitten from just a mere kiss. This is why it is so important to know yourself and play by your own set of rules. Just because your girlfriends can be casual about their hookups doesn't mean you can and should be, too. It's tough to restrain yourself when you really like someone, but remember to think beyond the hookup and ask yourself how you will feel the next morning. If you think your feelings will intensify but you are not quite sure about his, it's best to wait until you feel more confident about the relationship. When in doubt, keep holding out.

Chapter Four

HANDLING STICKY SITUATIONS

Yvette was madly in love with Dominic, her boyfriend of three months. She was finally certain she had found the love of her life. She thought Dominic was perfect in every single way . . . except one. He was always late. This wouldn't have been much of a problem if Yvette weren't the type who was always early. But she was. She liked making sure she had plenty of time to get where she was going and often buffered in a few minutes just in case something unexpected occurred. Being early allowed her to relax and enjoy what she was doing. Being late simply stressed her out.

One day, she and Dominic were headed to see a play. Yvette had bought the tickets weeks in advance and was very much looking forward to this particular performance. She asked Dominic if he could pick her up around four, giving them plenty of time to get to the theater and settle into their seats. He told her no problem. At 4:00, Yvette was outside her apartment waiting for Dominic. At 4:15, she was still waiting, so she texted him to see where he was. He apologized for being late as usual and said he would be there shortly. He finally arrived to pick her up at 4:30.

They got to the theater and found their seats just as the curtain opened. Yvette was extremely frustrated but didn't want to complain to Dominic because she was afraid he would think she was high maintenance and lose interest in her.

When I saw Yvette the following week, she expressed her frustrations. She was disappointed that Dominic had let her down and did not take her request to be on time seriously. When I asked her why she didn't say anything to him, she said she didn't want to be a nagging girlfriend and was afraid that he would think she was too demanding.

"I don't like confrontation," Yvette told me.

"No one does," I assured her. "But it is unavoidable in a relationship. If you lived in a bubble where nothing but the two of you existed, then maybe you could avoid conflict. But in the real world things happen and you have to be able to talk to each other, even when it's uncomfortable."

Yvette tried to reason with me. "But maybe I am making too big of a deal out of this. Shouldn't I pick and choose my battles? Shouldn't I let some things go?" she asked.

"Yes, you should, but because you are growing increasingly frustrated it doesn't seem like this is a battle you should surrender. Also, this is less about him being on time, and more about him respecting what you ask of him. Not telling him how you feel will lead you to resent him, and eventually you will begin to act out of resentment instead of love. You cannot hold this in because you are afraid he won't like you."

I made Yvette promise she would speak up next time Dominic's tardiness occurred. We practiced and role-played what she would say. The next time Yvette and Dominic went out, he was late again. Yvette mustered up all her courage and told Dominic how she felt. She explained how his behavior made her feel. She was not mean or angry, but she was not passive and meek either. She told him firmly, looking him directly in the eye, and she did not sugarcoat it with a smile.

After saying her piece Yvette felt like something was off. They were not quite in sync for the rest of the afternoon. She worried that what she said came off as abrasive and cold. She agonized and wondered if Dominic's feelings were changing. At one point she thought she should retract her statement and tell him she over-reacted, but she remembered I told her that if she did, it would only make things worse. They finished the date, and Dominic took her home.

The next morning, Yvette, who typically did not hear from Dominic on Mondays, woke up to find a very long e-mail from him waiting in her in-box. He apologized profusely for always making her late and expressed concern that *he* didn't want to lose *her!* He said he was sorry if he seemed out of sorts on their date, but he realized how much he truly loved being with her and hoped that she wasn't having doubts about him!

Yvette smiled as she read his words. She had made the right decision and the reaction was more positive than she could have hoped for. She heard from Dominic three more times that day—which made her even more certain she had done the right thing.

There is no way to escape occasional conflict in a relationship, no matter how much you like each other or how well you get along. There will be times when you or your guy does something foolish, thoughtless, or even contentious. How you react in these sticky situations can either keep your relationship moving forward on track or derail it completely. Therefore, it's best to know ahead of time ways to deflect or defuse some of these scenarios. In this

Was It Something I Said?

chapter we will talk about how to handle some of the stickiest situations, from what to do if you drink too much on a date and leave a bad impression to how to act if you unexpectedly run into your ex. How should you respond when your date says something rude or confusing, and what can you say if you make a big mistake and need to apologize?

The following are some of the most precarious dating situations with detailed advice on how to handle each of them.

How Should I React When He Cancels a Date?

Dear Jess,
    What do I say when a guy cancels on me? My last date cancelled on me with only an hour's notice. Should I act understanding even though I'm angry?

You spent the last three hours getting all dolled up, and now you have no place to go. Understandably, you are angry. You went through a lot of trouble to look good, and now your date has sentenced you to a night alone with your TiVo. But just because you feel angry inside doesn't mean you should take it out on your guy. In this case, the devil is in the details. How you react to his last-minute cancellation is going to depend on who he is, why he stood you up, and how he feels about it. To figure that out, answer the following questions as honestly as possible.

Did he A) stand you up for a good reason? For instance, he is out of town and his flight home was suddenly cancelled. Or B) give you some poor excuse, such as he is too hung over from partying the night before? Is he A) a guy that hardly ever cancels? Or is this

B) his typical flakey behavior? And last, is he A) sincerely sorry and dying to make this up to you? Or is he B) playing the victim by telling you he is forced to cancel but that it's not his fault?

If you answered all A's, then you should take the high road. You certainly can express your feelings to him, but identify what they really are first. You aren't actually angry. What you are is disappointed. Tell him that. Here is what you can say: "I'm sorry to hear about [his reason for cancelling]. I was really looking forward to seeing you, and naturally I'm disappointed we have to cancel, but I understand."

However, if you answered all B's, and you seem to always be last on the priority list, you may want to consider kicking this guy out of your funnel completely. He may not have the character for a real relationship. If he's constantly making and breaking plans with you, try saying this: "I'm very disappointed that you are cancelling again. Because this has happened a few times before, I can only assume this is going to happen again, and I'm not sure if I'm up for another letdown."

If he continually blames work, other people, or rotten luck for his unreliable behavior, it really does no good to point your wagging finger at him. Telling him he needs to do better will only prompt him to get defensive with you. Therefore, don't tell him what he's doing wrong; instead, tell him what action you are going to take because of what's transpired. Don't ask him to try harder; instead, explain to him that you can't date someone who continually changes plans at the last minute. Make a statement about you, versus directing demands at him.

My client Alyson learned the hard way that continuing to harp on someone's bad behavior never fixes anything. Almost from the very start, her new boyfriend Tommy proved to be unreliable. He made

Was It Something I Said?

lots of promises he never kept. He told her he would help fix her car, but he never did. He said he would pick her up from the airport, but he had something detain him at the last minute. He told her he'd pay her back when she lent him fifty bucks, but, of course, it slipped his mind. Each time Alyson was let down, she got angry and lectured Tommy on how to be responsible. The cycle repeated itself every two weeks, with Alyson having a major meltdown when Tommy broke a promise. Amazingly, after two months of dating, *he* was the one to break up with her, citing that she was too much like his mother.

If there is a shred of a decent guy in him, your man should straighten up and do better about keeping your dates—if you tell him what you need instead of making demands. If not, you'll just have to accept how he is if you want to keep seeing him (although I would strongly recommend finding a guy who is a man of his word instead).

How Do I Correct a Bad First Impression?

Dear Jess,

I did something very stupid. My friends set me up on a blind date, and because I was extremely nervous I had a few drinks beforehand. Then I became even more nervous when I saw my date, so I had a few more. By the end of the night I was very intoxicated. I'm worried I gave off a bad impression and won't hear from the guy again. Is there anything I can do or say to him to repair my sloppy image?

Believe it or not, there is a silver lining in this story. Typically people don't recognize that they have hit the bottle too hard and consequently affected their date. But you do! Acknowledging your actions is the most difficult part of the equation. Good for you for being self-aware (at least after the fact).

Drinking with someone you hardly know is risky. Consuming alcohol dulls the senses, making you less apt to care about other people's perception of you and allowing you to act without thought—the exact opposite mentality you should have on a first date when you are trying to impress someone! But I've beaten you up enough about this. Hopefully you understand now that drinking on a date is as precarious as drinking during a job interview. Now the question is, how do you recover and salvage your chances with this gorgeous, smart, and funny guy?

1. Admit your mistake.

Crying to your girlfriends while praying for him to call you won't fix anything. Take action and contact him yourself. Bypass the text and go straight for the call. He may not answer, so leave a message. Be honest. Tell him you have never been set up on a blind date before, so you were extremely nervous. Admit that you had a few cocktails beforehand to take the edge off and that clearly that was a big mistake. Then apologize for not being a better drunk (a little humor won't hurt).

2. Fight trashy with classy.

If your apology doesn't fix things, go one step further and fight the trashy image you left by doing something super classy. Tell him you'd like to make the whole thing up to him and take *him* out to dinner (or drinks) this time. After all, he did spend his money and time on you, and the real you wasn't even present. Don't beg him for another chance, simply say, "I'd really like the opportunity to make this up to you. Can I take *you* out to dinner this week?"

3. Move on.

If you go out again, don't mention your faux pas anymore. Telling him over and over again that it's not like you to get so drunk will lose its significance if you keep watering it down with apologies. Everyone makes mistakes; no need to keep recapping yours.

If he doesn't return your call or accept your offer, do not plot a recon mission to figure out how to win him back. You went on one date and it didn't work out. What is done is done. Move on to the next guy and carry this lesson on with you.

I'm Confused by What He Said. What Does He Really Mean?

Dear Jess,

This cute guy in my property law class finally asked me out! We had a great time together and he seems really into me. There was just one thing that confused me. At one point in the conversation he told me that he "isn't a normal guy" and that he "doesn't date." I am not sure what he meant by this. Do you know?

I get asked this question all the time. Not specifically what *your* date said, but I do get asked to interpret guy-speak quite often. Unfortunately, I'm still not fluent, even after years of date coaching. I have no idea what this guy meant. I have never met him and don't know his personality, so I couldn't tell you what "I don't date" means. It could suggest that he doesn't like to date and just wants to casually hook up. It could also mean that he doesn't like the uncertainty of dating and prefers the comfort of a relationship. The list of possibilities goes on and on. When you find yourself in a situation like this, there is one quick and easy way to decode his hidden meaning, and that is to simply ask the guy, "What do you mean?"

It sounds so obvious, but a lot of women are almost afraid to pose this question, as if you should know and understand him completely from day one—and to admit otherwise would be shameful. The truth is it takes a long time to get to know someone, and even after you've been together for a while, you will still have miscommunications from time to time. What he *says* and what you understand him to actually *be saying* can be very different.

When you ask the question, "What do you mean?" there will still be times when you won't get a clear answer. It sometimes happens that the response he gives won't satisfy you completely. Do not be afraid to ask again when this occurs. Dig! Get to the bottom of things. Don't just assume your own interpretation is correct. Get the resolution you need. Rephrase your question and ask again. You can say, "I'm not sure I fully understand what you are saying." Or you can reword your question into a statement to clarify his intent: "Are you saying that you . . . "

A client of mine, Julianne, was dating a guy for three months when they had their first relationship talk. Luke had recently been on travel for work, so they hadn't seen each other in a while. She started to worry that maybe they were losing their connection and that Luke was possibly dating someone else. When she

Was It Something I Said?

broached the subject of their relationship, Luke told her that they were not dating, but a step above that. Julianne wasn't sure what that meant. At the end of the conversation, she felt frustrated because she had not received the reassurance she wanted. After a few days, she decided to ask Luke what "a step above dating" was supposed to mean. To her surprise, Luke laughed and said he wasn't even sure himself! He said he guessed it was a step below a serious, committed relationship. Julianne, still unsatisfied with that response, answered, "I'm sorry, I don't know that stage at all. Can you explain to me what you mean?" That's when Luke told her he believed serious relationships were for people who had been together for several months and were moving toward marriage. Because they hadn't been together that long, he didn't think they were there quite yet. Then he added that he wasn't dating any other girls, was happy just being with Julianne, and could definitely see a future with her.

Don't feel silly for asking a guy to explain himself further. People often think they are being clear when, in fact, they aren't. Asking questions is a known sign of intelligence, so you have no reason to hold back or feel embarrassed. Show him how bright you are by really getting to know him.

Should I Call Him Out for Being Rude?

Dear Jess,

I was on a date the other night and got completely blindsided. The guy I was with commented several times on our waitress's large breasts. I thought it was pretty rude to be talking about another woman right in front of me. At the end of the date he asked me out for that weekend, and I didn't know how to respond! What should I have said? Should I give him a second chance? How do I handle rude men?

There are two ways to handle men with bad manners. The first way is to get through the date, say goodnight, and then delete their numbers from your phone. However, in many cases, you may really like the guy and, despite his inappropriate comment, want to see him again. Even good guys make mistakes sometimes. It's just the ones who learn from them when confronted that you want to keep around.

My friend Jackie went out with a guy from work that she was really into. While at dinner, and out of the office environment, she quickly learned how much he liked using the F-word in casual conversation. Everything he said was "f-ing" great or "f-ing" terrible. At the end of the date, Jackie was a bit turned off by all the profanity, but she still liked and wanted to see the guy again. I suggested she level with her date as soon as possible. If she didn't express how his cursing offended her, he would continue to use it and eventually the relationship would wear from it. I explained that when you have to have an uncomfortable conversation with someone, and you have to point out something he has done, the most important thing to remember is to *attack the problem, not the person.* Jackie told her date that she really liked him, but that she wasn't someone who used curse words or felt particularly comfortable hearing them. Her date apologized immediately and admitted that he didn't even realize he was swearing!

Let's say you decide that you do want to see your date again and want to tell him that his comments about the waitress made you uncomfortable. Start with a build and tell him that you enjoyed the evening with him. Then, if you want, you can prepare him for what you are about to tell him by saying, "I need to tell you something that made me uncomfortable tonight." This will forewarn him that you are going to address a serious concern. You don't want to attack him personally, so here is what you can say next: "I felt uncomfortable when you made that comment about the waitress." Or, "I was a little upset by those comments about the waitress."

After you tell your date how you feel in only one or two sentences, you should *remain silent for a minute* to let what you've said sink in and to allow your date to feel the uncomfortable-ness that you have felt throughout the night. Don't fill the silence with more talking. Let him hear you and be the next to say something. In most instances, the guy will apologize for his behavior, and you should accept it on the spot. But continue to evaluate whether he is in fact the right one for you.

You always want to refrain from directly telling your date he's rude or obnoxious, because in many cases his bad behavior will be unintentional. Besides, calling him out will only put him on the defensive. Therefore, even if he says or does something completely uncouth and your blood pressure flies off the charts, try to remain cool when you are delivering your message.

Should I Apologize for Yelling at Him in a Fit of Anger?

Dear Jess,

I did something bad. I have been dating a guy for six weeks, and after I slept with him I became a bit paranoid. One night he didn't return a text I had sent him. I logged on to G-chat, however, and saw him online. When he called me the next day, I got angry and told him he can't ignore me like that. I called him disrespectful and rude. He hasn't called since and I am starting to feel like I made a bad move. Can I call him? What should I say?

Yikes. I hope I never make you mad! Now that some time has passed, it sounds like you clearly see that you let your insecurity get the best of you. This guy may not have returned your text right away, but it doesn't mean he was intentionally ignoring you. Having sex with a guy before discussing exclusivity can do major damage to a girl's psyche. It creates high anxiety and causes you to worry unnecessarily. In this instance, your brain jumped to the worst-case scenario when your expectations were not met. You have to be careful not to put yourself in this kind of a position in the first place, but if you do, you have to know that lashing out at someone is the worst possible way to handle it.

My client Betty is one of the most attractive women I coach. When she walks into a room, everyone stops and takes notice. But Betty can't turn this God-given attention into a real relationship. Despite the many men she meets and goes out with, she continually gets dumped by all of them. The reason is that Betty gets angry when things don't go her way. The last guy she dated didn't call her early enough for a date. Instead of just not answering the phone to prove a point, or telling him that she had already made plans, she picked up and chewed him out for five minutes. Ironically, she even dropped a few curse words to emphasize how bad-mannered she thought he was. Terrified of ever getting that kind of a tongue-lashing again, the guy disappeared.

There is nothing scarier to a guy than an angry woman. They wonder if you get this angry over something small, what will

Was It Something I Said?

happen when life throws a real problem at you? Will your head rotate 360 degrees?

If you still like the guy and want to patch things up, it will be difficult to convince him that you really aren't as controlling and demanding as he thinks right now. Remember, a guy doesn't want to walk on eggshells and live in constant worry that he's doing something that will upset you, so you may have already sealed your fate. The only thing you can do in this circumstance is to call him or write him an e-mail and *throw yourself under the bus.* Take full responsibility for this occurrence. Apologize for losing your cool and tell him you are genuinely embarrassed by the way you acted. Tell him you don't blame him for not calling you back, because you wouldn't call yourself either. Close the conversation with, "I just wanted to say this because you are a really good guy and you didn't deserve to be talked to in that way. I wish you the best of luck in the future."

It's best that you don't leave things open-ended or ask him any questions. You want this call or e-mail to come across as a genuine apology and not as bait to get him to start chatting again.

That is all you can do for now. Will it get him to change his mind about being with you? It can't hurt to try. At the very least, it will help rebuild your good name in his eyes. It takes a big person to admit a mistake, so even though you lost your cool, owning up to it should balance things out. It will show him you are self-aware and able to take responsibility for your mistakes. Make sure you don't let too much time pass though. If you know you've done wrong, say so ASAP. Cauterize the wound quickly.

If the situation is more serious and your boyfriend has done something to genuinely upset you, go to page 199, *What Should I Say or Do When He's Upset Me?*

I Ruined My Chances with A Great Guy. Can I Win Him Back?

Dear Jess,

I ruined my chances with a great guy! We dated for three months, and I did everything wrong. I told him I loved him in the first few weeks, slept with him way too soon, and basically acted too needy throughout the entire relationship. When he broke up with me, he told me he just wasn't ready to commit, but I know it's because of all the mistakes I made. I know what I need to do better now, but I need him to give me a chance to prove it. Is there any way to talk him into taking me back?

As they say, you never get a second chance to make a first impression, and in your situation this man has already dated you, learned who you are, and decided that you are not compatible. Changing his mind about you now is not going to be easy. However, if you feel strongly about him and want to try, I do have some advice on how to best go about it.

1. Stop all contact.

I know this seems completely opposite from what you are trying to accomplish, but, for now, it's what needs to be done. The "needy, noncompatible you" is still fresh in this man's head. Any time you reach out to him in an attempt to show him you're different now won't do any good. Three months of bad behavior cannot be erased with one pleasant phone call or dinner date. Reconciliation will take time. Get comfortable, because it isn't going to happen by the weekend. A safe amount of time to wait would be half as long as the duration of your relationship. For

Was It Something I Said?

example, if you dated for three months, you should not contact him for a month and a half.

2. Disappear.

Much like the song "How Can I Miss You When You Won't Go Away," your ex can't miss you, or forget the way you were, if he continues to see you at the gym or bumps into you at the coffee shop in his office lobby. You must put time and distance between you. This means not only cutting contact directly (no texts, e-mails, phone calls), but also indirectly via Facebook, Twitter, or the occasional random run-in. He needs to wonder where you went, and he cannot do that if your status keeps popping up in his news feed.

3. Resurface.

Once you have let the recommended amount of time go by, you can then resurface. However, you should not contact your ex directly if possible. It would be better to casually connect again by running into each other randomly on purpose. The reason is that direct contact implies that you are not over the relationship and you are still attempting to make amends. And although that is the truth, your ex may be on guard if he feels that is the case. You want him to forget the past and see you in a whole new light. The reason he liked you in the first place was because when he met you, you were this confident, independent woman he had to win over. You didn't chase him. You let him chase you. Now you must do that again. When you see him, smile and be friendly. Tell him that he looks good and ask how he's been. Do not dive into any conversations about the past; rather, keep it light and easy. Show him the fun and relaxed side of you again. This is the time when you *act as if* you never had a prior relationship and behave as you would with someone you had just met. Flirt and be yourself. Do not linger for hours or go home with him! If he is still into you at all, he will slowly start to come around after this encounter. Remember to still *end your night at the Height of Impulse*, even if he begs you not to go. Take it as a good sign that a second chance could happen.

Bear in mind, however, that if you know your neediness drove him away the first time, you most likely have some work to do on yourself before trying to rekindle with him. Attempting to reactivate this relationship will be futile if you have not worked on your own self-esteem first.

Now if the situation is reversed and *he's* the one who's disappeared and then resurfaced on you, jump to page 115, *How Do I Handle a Run-in with My Ex?*

What Do I Do When His Words and Actions Are Inconsistent?

Dear Jess,

What does a girl do with a guy who is never consistent? My on-and-off boyfriend of two years has admitted before that he has never been consistent in a relationship. Recently, after being in a car accident, he called and told me he realized I was the love of his life and that he wanted to marry me. But then, as usual, I didn't hear from him for three days! When I finally called him, he told me he was stressed from work and I needed to be more understanding and give him space. I am so confused; why does he profess his love one minute and keep me at arm's length the next? How can I get him just to be consistent in his words and actions?

Was It Something I Said?

You may not realize it, but when you pose the question, "How can I get him just to be consistent in his words and actions," you are really asking how you can go about changing this man. I know you've probably heard this before, but you can waste a lot of time trying to change a man's behavior instead of just accepting who he is. After dating him for two years, I bet you can predict his every move by now. My advice is to stop fighting the obvious. Stop trying to understand him. You already do understand him. You just don't like who he is and you want him to be different. Being inconsistent (or "flakey," as I like to call it) is a personality trait much like having a short temper or a dry sense of humor. It's extremely difficult to change because it takes daily, self-motivated effort to improve. One car accident typically won't transform someone overnight, even if he said it did at the time. He made the promise without truly knowing what it would mean to keep it.

When you are dealing with men, *the best predictor of future behavior is in the past.* Your boyfriend has even admitted to never being consistent. This is a pivotal piece of information. If he has never been consistent in the past (with you or with anyone else), you can be quite certain he will never be consistent in the future.

My friend Celia was in love with Jack, her boyfriend of three years, but they fought quite often due to his socializing habits. Jack would frequently go out with his friends, forget to call Celia, and not come home until the following day. He was always apologetic and would have a great excuse for his behavior. Celia would threaten to break up with him, and Jack would swear that next time would be different. Of course, it never was.

Celia was confused as to why he would promise to change but never follow through. She assumed that if they got married, Jack would finally settle down. He would have to come home to her at night and be more accessible when he went out without her. They got engaged and married the following year.

On the night of their wedding, Celia told Jack that she was going to head back to the hotel room a few minutes ahead of him so she could change into something more comfortable. Jack told her he would follow right behind. She quickly changed and waited for her new husband so they could spend their first night together as a married couple.

But Jack never showed up.

Celia called his phone repeatedly, but it went straight to voice mail. She even went back out to the reception area to look for him. Finally she went to bed, completely devastated that Jack had disappointed her yet again. She woke up the morning after their wedding, in bed, alone. Jack had passed out in his best man's hotel room after the long night of celebrating.

Your on-and-off boyfriend sounds very similar to Jack, and, as you can see, not even marriage can fix someone's flakey ways. Although your man professes he will do better, he doesn't seem to want to put in the work necessary and he feels you'll accept the mere promise to change. To some extent he may be right. Have you found yourself getting angry at his behavior on some occasions but letting it go on others? Do you tell him you are done with the relationship but continue to see him? You, yourself, may be sending conflicting messages. If you threaten to leave but then accept his excuses and empty promises, how are you any different from him? You must be consistent in your words and actions, too. If you are unhappy with him and his behavior, merely making empty threats is not enough. You have to show him that there are consequences for unacceptable behavior and that jerking you around with promises of matrimony, and then telling you to give him space, is highly unacceptable.

As I mentioned in the "Hooking Up" section of this book, when a man frequently acts distant or vacillates between naughty and nice behavior, the best thing you can do is disengage. If you have already unsuccessfully attempted to talk things out in the past, saying what you have already said before will only reinforce that his bad behavior gets him attention. Instead of raising your voice and pointing out his problem for the fifteenth time, try not saying anything. Distance yourself from him. Teach him through your actions that you refuse this kind of treatment. The guy will quickly catch on and either improve on his own or push back on you. If he pushes back on you by blaming something or someone else for his behavior, then you can decide right then and there if that is the kind of marriage you want for the rest of your life. Any guy who doesn't take responsibility for his own actions is going to be a difficult one to live with.

Be sure to always tell a man why you are disengaging or behaving differently. Men are not mind readers, and if you don't tell them, "I'm upset because once again xyz happened," they will often blame the weather, the time of month, or some other guy-created theory. You don't have to explain yourself with a three-hour conversation either. Tell him with one or two sentences why you are upset and then let your actions do the rest.

One caveat: I don't recommend disengaging the first few times a particular problem arises. Talking things out is always the first and best way to resolve issues. However, if you cannot get through to your guy and you begin sounding like a broken record, this is usually a good secondary strategy.

What Is the Best Way to Handle Conflict When He's Angry with Me?

Dear Jess,

My boyfriend and I love each other a lot, but we fight all the time. When he gets upset with me, I usually start to cry or I just get defensive and yell back. At that point he usually stops arguing with me, but the fight always comes up again. Is there a way to handle conflict once and for all? I'm so tired of fighting.

Glad you are ready to tackle this problem! Most women shed a few tears when difficulties arise either purposefully or unintentionally, but you don't have to turn on the waterworks to ease the situation. In fact, handling conflict this way has clearly only perpetuated your problems. You have learned firsthand that what you don't fix now will only come back to haunt you later.

Conflict doesn't have to escalate into a full-on brouhaha. You both can voice your opinions without ending up in a screaming match. And handling it right the first time will help you avoid having to talk about it over and over again.

1. Let him vent.

When someone is upset with us, it's only natural to want him or her to stop being angry as fast as possible. We may either cry in the hopes of guilting him into giving up or jump in with our counter-remarks when he makes a point we disagree with. However, put yourself in the other person's shoes. If you were tying to express how you felt and the other person completely shut down or kept interrupting, how would that make you feel?

Although you may not want to hear his ranting, and although it may hurt your pride and your feelings, it is imperative that you let your partner vent his frustrations about you and the relationship (as long as he is doing it in a normal, healthy way). Even though you may want to refute every claim your boyfriend makes, don't. Let him talk. Let him vent it out. The reason this is important is because it is necessary to empty out all negative thoughts and frustrations so you start over with a clean slate. If you try to prevent him from venting, he will never feel like his side was heard, and therefore he will never be able to fully move on from the subject. So when you feel the urge to jump up and yell, "I object!" just take a deep breath and know that you will have your turn if you give him his.

Keep a notepad with you if you think you will forget your points. Jot them down when he is talking, but do not interrupt his train of thought.

2. Acknowledge that you heard him.

It may feel natural to ask, "Are you finished?" before launching into how you feel about all the gripes your man has about you. But fight the urge to dive into your own complaints the minute he's finished his closing arguments. If you really hate conflict, then you will not want to have this conversation again—so before taking your turn to speak your mind, tell your guy that you heard him. Keep engaged by looking him in the eye, nodding your head yes (not in agreement necessarily, but to let him know you are hearing him), and. above all else, avoid any eye-rolling! Letting him vent is more than just sitting there while he rants; it's about letting him know you are listening to his feelings even if they make you uncomfortable. If you roll your eyes, however, you are subconsciously telling him you think his points are invalid.

Here are some examples of what you can say to let him know you heard his side:

- I can see why you would say XYZ.
- I hear what you are saying about my XYZ.
- Let me just repeat what I heard so I am sure I understand your side. . .

Half the time you may realize that what he said and what you heard are completely different. That is why this is also an important step. It allows your partner to feel like you listened, but it allows you to make certain you understand him.

3. Tell him how you feel about what he's said and be open to the fact that you may need to do better.

Whether you agree or disagree, it is important for you to speak up and say how you feel. You aren't perfect, so try to suppress your ego from fighting your point just to make yourself right. If you can agree to a little self-improvement, the fight should be over. If you are going to make a counterpoint, however, be careful of the words you choose. Remember to *attack the problem and not the person.* You can either use *Feel–Felt–Found* to make your case, or you can use a simple "I feel" statement.

"You" statements blame the other person, and, if you use them, you may end up back at step one again. Here are some examples of how to turn "you" statements into "I feel" statements:

You obviously don't care about me!
I feel as if you don't care when you say . . .

You are just as much to blame as I am!

I feel like this is something we both have to work on together. Do you agree?

You are never happy with anything!

I feel as if I don't make you happy. Is that true? What can I do better?

Keeping these three steps in mind will help you quickly maneuver your way through the uncomfortable parts of the conversation and steer you toward resolution. Remember that if your boyfriend is upset with you, it's best you hear about it rather than avoid it. A healthy relationship requires both parties to constantly grow and evolve, so don't be afraid of a little constructive criticism from your partner. Running for cover or defusing him with tears won't solve the problem. In fact, it usually will just add fuel to the next fire.

How Do I Handle a Run-in with My Ex?

Dear Jess,

I have not heard from the guy I am dating in almost three weeks. I know that I am going to see him tonight, because my friend's birthday is being held at his favorite club. What do I do when I see him? Ignore him? Ask him why he hasn't called?

This may be the Grand Poobah of sticky situations: the dreaded run-in with an ex! (And yes, if he hasn't called you in three weeks, you are no longer dating and he has become your ex.) Although this scenario tops the awkward chart, it does not have to be an agonizing experience. Handled correctly, you can deal with the situation and still have a wonderful night out with your friends.

While ignoring him is a popular strategy among scorned women, it has one very unpleasant downside. It usually inhibits you from having a fun night because you are so consumed with avoiding him. Rather than being on guard for the next four or five hours, diffuse the situation by going right up to your ex and saying hello. Don't wait for the perfect time, because there isn't one. Don't wait for him to come to you, because he most likely won't. Taking the initiative and approaching him sends the message that you are mature enough to remain friends regardless of what happened between you. Here is what you should say:

> *You:* Hi there. I saw you when I walked in and just wanted to say hello. How have you been?
> *Him:* (Feeling like a complete jerk) Uh, I'm good. How are you?
> *You:* I'm great, thanks. I'm just here for so-and-so's birthday party. I don't know if you met her before or not. Anyway, it was nice seeing you. I have to get back to my friends now. Have a good night.

Two things will happen after you complete this mission. One, you will be able to enjoy yourself for the rest of the evening, and, two, you will show your ex that he doesn't have a hold on you. If he is at all still interested, this play will allow him to approach you again later in the night and if that does happen, you must put him on the spot for his sudden disappearing act. You can't call him out if you approach him, but if he comes on to you, you have to stand up for yourself. Here is what you say:

Him: (Obviously flirting) You look nice tonight, I like that dress. Yada, yada, yada, we are all headed to another bar after this, do you want to come?

You: I'd like to, but we have not talked in almost three weeks. What's been going on with you? (Or) What happened to you?

Him: I've just been busy.

You: And . . .[*not said condescendingly but inquisitively*]

Him: And I know I should have called you but I was afraid you wanted something serious and I am not sure what I want yet.

You: What made you think that?

From there you can hear him out and then decide if you want to retreat or rekindle the relationship. Most of the time if someone has disappeared on you, he is prone to doing it again. Therefore, be cautious if you give this romance a second chance.

Why Can't I Hold On to a Guy?

Hi Jess,

I have a serious problem that I don't know how to fix. Men are always asking me out, but after a few dates they tell me they aren't ready for anything serious and just want to date casually. How can that be? When they approach me they seem extremely interested but then something happens and they completely change their minds. What is going on?

A man who finds you attractive will come on as strong as a politician campaigning for your vote. When in pursuit mode, a guy is solely thinking about how to get you to say yes to a date. Because men are visual, attraction goes a long way—and how nice for you that many of them like what they see! However, there does come a point in all courtships where physical attraction loosens its grip and your other qualities are factored into his feelings for you. Getting to this point generally takes between a few weeks and a few months. The fact that you are repeating such a strong pattern indicates you are either subconsciously picking the worst potential matches for yourself or you are demonstrating one of the two universal relationship turnoffs. Regardless of how good you may look on the outside or how hard he has pursued you before, if you display one of these fatal characteristics, you will constantly find yourself back on the market time and time again.

1. *You are unknowingly desperate.*

You may have a bevy of fantastic qualities, but your need for security is so great that it unfortunately supersedes every one of them. Perhaps you've been burned in the past so you are always anticipating something going wrong. Or you are so focused on landing a boyfriend it's almost become your second job. Either way, if you are so concerned with where this new relationship is going, you won't be able to enjoy where it is right now. If you think that every date should result in a lasting relationship, you are most likely putting unnecessary stress on yourself and your guy. That stress then translates to pressure, and we all know what pressure can do to a man.

Stop trying to control the future and instead just appreciate and enjoy the date you are on. Fight the urge to rush the relationship by continuing to *fill your funnel* with other dates. The more options you have, the less you will stress. If you are the type who gets easily attached after just one kiss, *hold back that Bullet* until you know that this guy has long-term potential. Most important, remember that not all dates are meant to go the distance, and it doesn't mean you've failed at love. Some men will not be good matches, and if you stopped worrying for a few minutes you would probably see that a lot more clearly.

2. Your expectations are too high.

He took you to a chain restaurant, didn't notice your haircut, and forgot to let you order first. Your good mood has soured and you feel like asking this guy why you are even out on this date when he's clearly not that into you. Or is he? Could it be perhaps that you had a certain, very specific kind of treatment in mind and are disappointed by your own self-conjured expectations? Before you spend the next two hours sulking over your Bang-Bang Chicken, ask yourself if maybe *you* are the one who needs lessons in dating.

If you are frequently annoyed, irritated, upset, or angry with the guys you date, you may be expecting too much or placing too much importance on frivolous things. Being a negative or nitpicky Nelly is a guaranteed way to drive a man out the door and into the arms of someone else. You don't want to compromise your core values and you should continue to look for red flags, but his taking you to The Cheesecake Factory and overlooking that half-inch trim are not considered punishable crimes.

No man feels good about disappointing his woman, so if you continually seem unhappy and ungrateful, it's not surprising that your dates give up on you after a while. Instead of focusing on what he did wrong or what he could have done better, appreciate him for who he is and what he is currently doing to make you happy. Men are not given a handbook on how to date. They try the best way they know how. You aren't required to love all their ideas, but you should appreciate the motivation behind them.

If you aren't guilty of any of the previous charges, then you could in fact be investing all the right energy into all the wrong guys. They may not be jerks or players—just not the right fit for you. A guy may court you with all the right moves in the beginning, but if the relationship doesn't seem to progress as more time passes, you have to ask yourself if the connection is really there. If you have been dating someone for three months but don't feel any closer to him than you did on date three, the answer is probably not. Physical chemistry is not enough. There must be an emotional bond as well. If it's not there after a few months, you should cash in your chips and move on. Drop the "got-to-make-this-work" mind-set because, if you don't, every guy will eventually drop you. Accepting the fact that this guy isn't *the* guy and moving on to someone else will save you a lot of time and even more heartache. Keep in mind that only one man will work out, so it's perfectly normal for the other 99 percent not to!

Some situations are stickier than others, but no matter what awkward circumstance plays out on your dates, you have only two choices: address it or ignore it. If you address it, do so in the most appropriate and tactful way. If you choose to ignore it, be very certain you aren't doing so merely to avoid an uncomfortable situation. Turning a blind eye to a guy's odd or unacceptable behavior

Was It Something I Said?

can often lead to bigger problems down the road. If you think you are being agreeable and easygoing by not speaking your mind, think again. Easygoing means not caring if he orders Thai or Chinese for dinner, not repressing your core beliefs. Men can very quickly gauge that you are sacrificing your own needs to appease them, and they will not see you as being thoughtful or considerate when you do this. They see the truth: that you are scared and unsure of yourself. And there is nothing attractive about that.

Chapter Five

SOCIAL NETWORKING

From the way she was talking, you would have thought the world was ending. I was on the phone with Liz, a twenty-four-year-old graduate student. She had met Nathan, a smart but shy IT consultant, three weeks ago and they had gone on five dates. The last time they saw each other, Nathan had told her he wasn't dating other girls and wanted to see where their relationship would lead. So far he had been consistent, following up after each date and sending her texts during the week. Typically, he reached out to her every other day—that is, until after their fifth date.

Liz was a mess. Nathan had let two days go by without sending so much as a text message. She was so excited to have met someone that the thought of losing him so quickly was unbearable. Like a detective, she analyzed everything from their last date, searching for any clues to help figure out why Nathan had backed off. Everything checked out. Not even a slight hiccup was present. We were both scratching our heads. When I finally saw her a day later, she burst into my office with her laptop in tow and told me she had finally figured things out.

"It's worse than I thought," Liz exclaimed. "After our last date, Nathan had friend-requested me. I was actually a bit hesitant to add him because our relationship is so new, but I didn't want to seem rude, so I accepted. I just went on his page, and look what's posted!"

Liz turned the screen toward me. The post on Nathan's page was from a pretty brunette. It read, *Hey Hot Stuff! See you later tonight—looking forward to it!*

"Who is this girl, Jess? Her page is completely private so I don't know anything about her. Do you think he's going out with her? Has he lost interest in me? Should I call him and ask who the heck this is?" Liz looked so distraught I thought she might start to cry.

I tried to calm her down, saying, "Listen, I don't know who this is, but I do know that Nathan friend-requested you only a few days ago. If he was seeing someone else, he would not have done that."

Liz chewed on her nails in a panic. "But what if he just met her? Girls are fast these days! I haven't heard from Nathan since Monday and it's now Wednesday. It is not like him to wait this long. I think he is going out with this girl. I really want to post a comment under her comment. Maybe something like, 'Hope you and Hot Stuff have a good one!'" she said rashly.

"Liz, I know you're upset and confused, but try to remember that it hasn't been that long since you last heard from Nathan. It's still early and you may hear from him today. Did you two talk about plans to do something this coming weekend?" I asked.

"Yes, we talked about going on a long bike ride all the way out to Leesburg," she said.

"Great. Here is what you can do. I would wait until tomorrow and if you haven't heard from him, it would be fine to call Nathan and ask what time he wants to meet for the bike ride. Because you are now in an exclusive relationship, you can take a little bit more initiative. I want you to say to him, 'Hey, I was just calling to check in and see how you are doing. We still on for the bike ride?' If something is wrong, you will be able to tell from the tone of his voice. Then you can probe further. But for now, I want you to assume everything is fine between you. Don't jump to conclusions just yet."

Liz nodded that she understood. Even though she was feeling impatient about the situation, she promised she would not do anything until the next day. As she got up to gather her things, her phone went off. Immediately her face lit up.

"Jess! It's a text from Nathan! He says he's thinking about me and can't wait to hang out this weekend," she said with mixed emotion.

Then her phone went off again.

"Oh my gosh!" Liz exclaimed. "He just wrote that his ex-girlfriend had her friend post on his wall trying to cause us problems. He hopes if I saw it, it didn't upset me," she said.

"There you have it. Mystery solved. It sounds like he's open to talking about it too, which is great," I told her.

"I'm just so relieved! Thank you for keeping me calm, Jess. I'm so glad I didn't do or say anything about this to him first."

She headed for the door with a renewed sense of confidence.

"Liz," I called after her. "In the future, it may be best not to accept a friend request so soon."

"I know. I wouldn't have requested him, but I thought it would be mean if I didn't accept his request. You don't think it seems rude to ignore someone like that?" she asked.

"I think if you have to choose between ignoring a request and exposing yourself to information like this too soon, you are better off with the former. At least you can control that option," I told her.

Liz nodded in agreement and then hurried out the door.

Was It Something I Said?

Since its inception, social networking has done dating a world of help as well as a world of hurt. Sites like Facebook provide us with a wonderful way to connect with friends and old flames, but they also have had a hand in evoking jealousy, aiding infidelity, and creating general misunderstandings. Therefore, they must be used with great care. Before the creation of social networking sites, you never knew what people were doing unless they told you. Now, not only can you tail people from the comfort of your own home, thanks to status updates, you even have access to what thoughts they are thinking. It's crazy to have so much inside information . . . and sadly, it's making some of us even crazier.

Although you think you may want to know everything about the man you are seeing, there are some things that you shouldn't be privy to early on. Most of us are gluttons for punishment, however, and we just can't seem to scrounge up the discipline to turn a blind eye, so we learn things we should not know. Then our judgment becomes influenced, and we can ultimately make bad decisions from it. What then do we do with this inside information? How do we handle situations that, a few years ago, never would have existed? Today's relationships can live and die on the pages of a social networking site; therefore, we must learn how to carefully handle some of the contentious events that too often lead to catastrophe. In this chapter we will discuss the most frequently asked questions relating to our social network. What do you do if you discover the guy you are dating lied about his whereabouts? Do you have the right to say something? Can you ask your new boyfriend to take down pictures of his old girlfriend? How do you get someone to change their status to "in a relationship," and what if he refuses to do so? The following are the most common social networking questions with detailed advice on how to handle each of them.

Should I Add Him As a Friend on Facebook?

Dear Jess,

There is this guy at school that I want to talk to, and I'm pretty sure he's noticed me, although I can't be certain of it. I wanted to add him as a friend on Facebook in hopes that maybe he would start to talk to me. I was wondering if that was a good idea. Thanks!

It's not a bad idea; however, it would be an even better idea to strike up a conversation first in person. If you randomly add him out of the blue, he's going to know you are interested in him. Why else would you add a guy you haven't met? Then the mystery and challenge of winning you over will be greatly reduced. Plus, adding him as a friend now will likely prompt you to cyber-stalk him, and, as I said before, you may learn things that could wrongly influence your judgment of this guy. The best strategy in this instance is to try to get to know this person offline first. Even if you can manage to run into him once and have a short "warm-up" conversation, it will be better than adding him cold. If you friend him after that, it will seem more like a natural progression of your relationship and, if he is interested at that point, he may take advantage of your new connection by sending you a message.

How Do I Strike Up a Conversation with Him First?

The best way to strike up a conversation with this guy, or anyone for that matter, is to use an *Icebreaker*. An *Icebreaker*, or *IB* for short, is a small, casual remark that usually pertains to something in your present surroundings. For example, if you are out shopping at the mall and you spot this guy, you could joke that the music being played in stores now makes you feel like you are at a night-club. Or if you are at a coffee shop standing in line next to him, you could tell him you are feeling adventurous and ask if he knows what is in a Caramel Macchiato. You don't need to come up with a witty or profound opening statement. Most guys will just be happy that you are talking to them at all, and they will continue the conversation if they are interested.

You can also use a compliment as an *IB* to open the conversation. If you see him playing with the newest electronic device, tell him how envious you are of his new toy and ask how he likes it. You could also compliment a unique piece of clothing on him. Everyone loves compliments, and guys don't get nearly enough.

If you have seen him around, either at school or work, you can go one step further and actually introduce yourself if you are fairly sure he's noticed you, too. Get in line for lunch next to him or follow him into the elevator. When he looks at you, smile. Then say, "I feel like I see you around a lot. My name is ____." Because you attend the same school or work at the same place, it isn't odd for you to introduce yourself. It's just being friendly.

After you have done all this, then you can add him on Facebook. But the smarter thing to do is to wait and see if he adds you first. If he wants to know you better, chances are good that he will. Wait a few days at the very least to give him the opportunity to make a move on you first. Remember though, timing is almost everything when it comes to making a first impression and cultivating a new relationship. A man has to be interested in you to ask you out, but he also has to be physically, mentally, and emotionally available. If he just broke up with someone and is hurting over that relationship, for instance, it won't matter how cute you looked the day you met him. But just because something doesn't happen right away does not mean it won't ever happen at all.

Can I Post a Comment Thanking Him for Our Date?

Dear Jess,

I've gone out with a guy three times and I'm crazy about him. He's really cute, so I worry that other girls may like him, too. Because we just had a date, can I post a thank-you note on his Facebook page just to let all the women out there know that he is taken?

As we discussed before, the guy should be the one to follow up after a date, not you. Texting him a thank-you note tells him how much you like him; posting a thank-you note on his wall tells the whole world. Although you may frighten some women away, you also could scare him off in the process. If he is dating other girls (which is allowed at this stage, so he's not really taken yet), he could find your little scheme annoying, especially if it causes trouble for him. Don't let your insecurities talk you into making a bad decision. Be a classy girl and don't worry about who else is vying for his attention. You are the one he's dating, after all!

Was It Something I Said?

I don't recommend posting pictures, either. As the saying goes, a picture is worth a thousand words, and it's obvious what you are trying to say here. Posting a photo of the two of you is almost more aggressive than the "thank-you" wall post. If you spend too much energy worrying about other girls stealing this guy away, you will ultimately sabotage your chances for a relationship with him. If you let fear run your brain, it will drive you in the wrong direction every time. Don't post anything on this man's wall. Wait for him to post on yours first.

If a guy tells you to let him know when you post pictures of the two of you, then it is obviously safe to do so. Beyond that, it really is better to wait until you are in a relationship to do any posting or tagging of pictures of the two of you together. Use Shutterfly or some other private photo sharing site in the meantime.

How Do I Get Him to Change His Status to "In a Relationship"?

Dear Jess,

The guy I have been dating for eight weeks has his relationship status set to single. How do I get him to change it to "in a relationship"? Can I change mine first and hope he follows my lead?

These days, it seems the true testament of a man's feelings are not in his words or actions, but rather are laid out on his Facebook page. Most women claim that until their guy announces to the world that he is "in a relationship," they just can't be sure where the relationship stands. If you have not yet had the "relationship talk," changing your status before discussing exclusivity is a sure-fire way to get your man to freak out. Before you start worrying about your online status, make sure you determine the grounds of your relationship in person. See page 181, *How Do I Bring Up the "Relationship Talk"?*

If you have been dating for several months and your guy has told you that he is committed to you, there is no reason he should have a problem changing his status, *if he is in fact a frequent Facebook user.* Some guys spend little time on and put little stock in social networking sites, and they are simply unaware that they are still cyber-single. I would not change your status first in the hopes your guy will follow suit. I would talk to him first and plan to change it together.

If enough time has passed where your guy has had a chance to change his status on his own but hasn't yet, tell him you feel silly having your status set to single when you are so happily involved with him. Tell him you think you are going to change yours and ask him if he wouldn't mind changing his, too. It should be no problem for him if he's serious about you. If he gives you a reason as to why he doesn't want to switch his status—for instance, he doesn't like broadcasting his business to the world—you want to *Trust but Verify* his statement. As I said before, some men are not frequent Facebook users and do not like having their life documented online. Take him at his word, but verify that this explanation is consistent with his other beliefs. If he doesn't like being tagged in pictures, never updates his status line, and refrains from wall posts, then you should accept his reasoning. Do not push him or throw a tantrum to get your way. Some people are more discreet than others, and, if your boyfriend is one of them, you have to respect that and find a middle ground.

Was It Something I Said?

However, if you are dealing with a serial status updater and the only area this man keeps private is his relationship status, he could have an ulterior motive for keeping you a secret. One of my clients had been dating a club promoter for six months who kept his status at single until my client asked him to change it. He told her he didn't want to draw attention to himself or their relationship. To appease her, he agreed to leave his marital status blank altogether. This satisfied my client for a few months until she realized her boyfriend was updating his page daily, posting group pictures of all his friends, but never once did he allude to dating someone. One day he left his profile up, and she realized he was using Facebook to meet other girls.

Do keep in mind that once you change your relationship status, unless you get married, you will have to change it back at some point. Then the whole online world will know that you and your man have parted ways. So make sure you are really serious about each other before you go public.

Can I Call Him Out about a Wall Post?

Dear Jess,

The guy I recently started seeing went out last night and didn't tell me. The only reason I know is because a friend of his posted a comment on his page about it. I am really angry now. Can I call him out on this? I feel like he totally screwed up and I caught him!

Maybe I am misreading you, but it sounds like you are actually enjoying that you caught this man doing something wrong. Are you itching to tell him off for some reason? If you have a history with him and he has wronged you before, I would understand why this would be upsetting; however, you said you recently started seeing him, which tells me not enough time has passed for you to have any major complications yet. Therefore, you have to be careful that you are not mixing anger from a past relationship into your present one. If you are not even his girlfriend yet, is he really obligated to tell you what he's doing all the time? Is it possible that he thought he would be staying in, but his friends coerced him into joining them out on the town? Before you let your emotions drive you over to his house to rip his head off, why not wait and see if he owns up to going out? Perhaps when you see him he will mention that one of his buddies persuaded him into doing something. If he comes clean and doesn't have anything to hide, will you still be angry that he didn't pick up the phone and tell you about his change of plans? That may be asking a lot of someone you've only been dating a few weeks.

Your guy is more likely to tell you the truth about his whereabouts *if you approach him in a friendly, non-accusing way.* When you get together, maintain your typical, congenial demeanor. Warm up the conversation by talking about neutral subjects: his life, work, or anything else going on with him. This will allow him to relax and let down his guard (if he has one up). Then in a very nice, calm way ask, "Did you end up doing anything last night?" He should tell you exactly what happened because, judging from your calm disposition, he will see that you aren't upset and there is no reason to hide anything. People lie to avoid getting in trouble, so if you give him no indication that you are angry, he is more apt to just speak the truth. Although you may want to come at him with guns blazing and an angry attitude, remember that approach will more likely cause him to lie, shut down, or inwardly make the decision to stop dating you because you are downright scary.

If you want to get the real story out of a guy regarding his whereabouts, his past, or any controversial topic, you must approach him in a friendly, noncombative way. You will catch more bees with honey than you will with death threats. A man will open up if he feels he can do so without being attacked. Once you get the truth, you can then decide if you like his answer or not. But beware: No guy is going to want to be your boyfriend if a relationship with you is like being under house arrest. You want to be a guy's partner, not his parole officer.

If you are having trouble getting your boyfriend to open up in general, jump to page 194, *How Do I Get Him to Open Up about His Feelings?*

If your guy continually lies to you about where he's been, that's another story. There is no reason to keep dating someone who lies to you for any reason. Lying indicates selfishness and is also a sign of weakness. Get back out there and find yourself a man who is strong enough to speak the truth.

Can I Post My Feelings on Twitter in Hopes That He Sees It?

Dear Jess,

My boyfriend and I are going through a rough patch. He told me that he doesn't think we are right for each other and that he can't make me happy. I'm pretty upset about it, and he won't talk to me because he says we need time and space apart. I don't know what to do but I'm going crazy not talking to him. Can I post my feelings on Twitter in the hopes that he sees it?

Let's walk through this situation step by step so we can really understand why tweeting your emotions is the worst idea you've ever had. Sorry that was harsh, but I want to hammer home how much I disapprove of this and illustrate why posting your misery is only making matters worse for you.

Although he didn't use the exact words, your boyfriend broke up with you. And when a guy breaks up with a girl, there is always a huge amount of guilt that comes with the territory. He doesn't want to see you cry. He doesn't want to feel like the biggest creep on the planet. As if having the break-up conversation wasn't bad enough, now he is going to be constantly reminded of the anguish and despair he's caused every time he logs online and sees your updates. If you want him to miss you and even remotely regret ending things, guilting him and making him feel like a jerk is not the way to do it.

Think about how you feel when people you know, friends or family members, use guilt to get you to do something for them. Does it make you *want* to do what they are asking? Do you feel excited and happy to help when they guilt you? Or do you begin to resent and dislike them for making you feel bad? This is what you are doing to your ex, and you are only driving him further away by continuing to air your affliction on Twitter or any other social networking site.

I know venting to your many followers might make you feel better, as it can be therapeutic to get your feelings out and have your friends post their support, but you have to think about the long-term effects of your actions. If you really want a chance to patch things up with your boyfriend, you have to stop the emotional posting and remember he asked for time and space, which in truth you are not giving him right now.

A great way to feel better and not affect your chances of reconciliation with your ex is to write him a letter. Tell him everything you are thinking and feeling. Do not censor it. Just let it pour out of you. Get as mad, sad, hurt, or frustrated as you want. Then put the letter in a safe place, because you are not going to send it. You don't have to have your ex read it for you to feel better. The next time you feel the urgent need to talk to him again, take out another piece of paper. Writing him letters is just as cathartic as posting your thoughts online, but it has no consequences. Give it a try. You can, of course, reach out to your family and friends if you need to vent or want extra support; just make sure you do it offline.

When a man says he needs time apart to think, or space to sort out his feelings, what he is trying to tell you is that you have smothered him. *You did not do it on purpose, but, nonetheless, it happened.* Therefore, the last thing you want to do is keep smothering him by trying to contact him either directly by phone or e-mail, or indirectly by Twitter. Let him feel his freedom and taste his independence instead. If he really loves you and you're right for each other, he will begin to miss you and the joy and comfort you bring to his life. But he cannot miss this if you don't go away.

Should I De-friend Him?

Dear Jess,

I met a guy one night and he friend-requested me the next day on Facebook asking me out for a drink. I agreed, but he never followed through. About two weeks later I e-mailed him and asked if he still wanted to get together. No response! I'm so angry and confused. I feel like an idiot for saying yes to the date. Should I de-friend him?

It's beyond frustrating when you think a man is interested in you and then he completely disappears without warning. It can drive you crazy trying to solve the mystery of what happened. Luckily, I have cracked the case! The strongest piece of evidence here is that he abruptly lost interest without seeing or even speaking to you again. Assuming you didn't have any unsavory pictures or wall posts for him to question, there is only one real explanation for this: There is another girl involved. He either has a girlfriend, or he has at least been casually dating someone for a while. The question now is why did he reach out to you? Usually it is because at the time you met him, his relationship was on the rocks, but not too long after things improved. That's why he came on strong within the first twenty-four to forty-eight hours of meeting you, but after a few days passed you didn't hear from him again.

This scenario actually happens quite often. It even happened to me before I was married. In *You Lost Him at Hello,* I tell my own similar story of a guy who friended and flirted with me but never asked me out. A few weeks later I ran into him and his girlfriend at a restaurant. With a little research I learned they had been together for two years when he contacted me. They had broken up for a week, but then promptly got back together.

Guys like these may pop back into your life sporadically when you least expect it, but you can bet your bottom dollar it's because he and his girlfriend are on the outs again. You should not feel foolish for agreeing to the date. This guy wasn't trying to test you or play a trick on you. He thought you were attractive and if he wasn't already attached, you'd probably be sipping a cocktail with him right now.

Was It Something I Said?

De-friending the guy is a personal choice. If it irritates you to see his status updates or know that he can view your page when you really don't know him that well, then unfriend him. He may be a little shocked when he realizes you've done this, but do you really care what he thinks at this point? I know. Yes, you do care. That's why you wanted to unfriend him in the first place, to send a message loud and clear that he can't ask you out and not follow up. I will tell you honestly, and this may make you feel better or worse, that he is not thinking about you right now. He has a life and lots of other worries. In fact, he may not even notice that you de-friended him, because it's not like there's any obvious indication when this happens unless he tries to view your page. He's not sitting behind his laptop laughing at how he dumped you before he even got to know you. He's moved on for now, and you should do the same. I know you are disappointed and your ego may be a bit bruised, but slap a bandage on it and get back out there. If this is the worst thing to happen to you this year, consider yourself a lucky woman.

If you are really, really interested in this guy and want to leave the door open for him to reach out in the future, then leave him be and hide his updates so you don't have to see them. You may hear from him again in the future if and when his current relationship ends for good. Remember, timing, timing, timing!

How Do I End a Facebook War with My Ex?

Dear Jess,

I cannot get over my ex-boyfriend. Just as I begin to feel like I'm getting over him, he somehow reels me back in. I probably visit his Facebook page twenty times a day. I do try to make him jealous by having other guys post on my Facebook wall, and he does seem to respond to that. This has been going on for six months now, and I know we either need to get back together or move on, but for some reason we are just stuck in the same place. What can I say to him to get him to make a decision about us?

As the saying goes, it takes two people to start a relationship but only one to end it. In your case there is only one way for you to push things along. You can move on, because you don't need your ex's consent to do that. And that is what you're waiting for, isn't it? For your ex to tell you whether you are getting back together, or for him to give you permission to move on. I hate to say this, but he's not going to do either. It's up to you at this point to decide what you want to do. Don't look to your ex for direction. He doesn't have any himself, as evidenced by his own behavior.

If you feel you need one last-ditch effort with this guy, try reaching out to him and saying, "I can't keep doing this back and forth with you. It's unhealthy for us both. I think it's best that we don't communicate for a while if we are going to remain broken up."

The "if" in that sentence is key. If your ex wants to get back together, that word will give him the slight opening he needs. At the same time, you are keeping your dignity by alerting him that you will be making serious changes from this point forward.

If at that point he says he can't decide, it's because he's torn. He doesn't want to lose you, but he doesn't want to commit to you either. This is extremely common. The only thing to do if your ex is indecisive is make the decision for him. Tell him you have to move on. If he really loves you and wants to try again, *the fear of loss you invoke by walking away will prompt him to come after you.* Erase his number from your phone and, more important, de-friend him on Facebook and every other site that connects you. The reason you have not been able to move on from limbo is because you are still in contact with each other. Even on the days when you don't speak to him directly, you are tracking him online, which is keeping you involved in this relationship. Although you may like that you can keep tabs on him, it's the primary reason you have not gotten over him. Cut all communication and you will start to become unstuck. Do not worry about his reaction to this. De-friending is not rude or mean, because you've already told him you will be making changes. If he gets mad or says you are being childish for going to this extreme, know that he is really upset by the loss of control he used to have on you, not because you de-friended him.

Moving on is a lot easier said than done, but you must let go of the happy past relationship that you want back and accept your relationship as it stands right now. Right now it isn't healthy, and you need to base your decisions on your relationship today, not six months or a year ago.

If your boyfriend tells you that he absolutely does not want a relationship with you, but still continues to call and see you, jump to page 187, *Why Does He Say We Aren't in a Relationship?*

What Should I Do If My Boyfriend Is Jealous of My Facebook Friends?

Dear Jess,

My boyfriend flips out on me whenever another guy posts a comment on my wall. I have a lot of guy friends I grew up with and he can't seem to get over it. He wants me to take down my whole page. I don't know how to get through to him that I would never cheat and he has nothing to worry about. Do you have any advice on what to say to him?

It doesn't matter how much you reassure your boyfriend of your fidelity. The core issue here is not that you have too many guy friends and he doesn't trust you; the problem is that your boyfriend is insecure. If he is relatively young, does not have much experience with women, and hasn't been with you for very long, it may be something he will grow out of with time. However, if his teenage years are long behind him, you have been dating for a while, and have no prior record of being unfaithful, this problem could get bigger as time goes on.

The question comes down to this: How serious are you about your boyfriend? Is he the one? Do you think you are going to marry him? If the answer is unequivocally yes, then you both may want to consider taking down your pages or making a combined page so that you both have access. This may help calm your boyfriend's nerves. I can't stress enough, though, that this option is only for couples who intend to marry. If you are both still in college, for example, and you have not yet experienced the real world, then this is not the best route to go. It is important to maintain your own social life in your teens and twenties, and Facebook is a great facilitator in helping with that. You don't want to shut out your friends just because your boyfriend is self-conscious and angry.

Try asking your man if there is something else you can do that would make him less apprehensive about your male friends. Perhaps you can use a picture of the two of you as a profile picture?

Was It Something I Said?

Or maybe post a sweet comment on his page every day for a week. Sometimes the best way to fight jealousy and insecurity is not to subtract things, but to add. Make sure you genuinely show appreciation for your boyfriend, not just when he's feeling down, but every day. As women, we can sometimes forget that men need reassurance, too. Make a daily effort to compliment him on something. Not just on his physical appearance but on the more substantial things—his humor, his wit, or his warm heart.

If none of this helps, and you feel that your boyfriend is simply too controlling and wants you all to himself, you may be in an unhealthy and potentially dangerous relationship. You have the right to have friends, so do not let your boyfriend make you think otherwise. If he is also controlling on a number of other issues, don't be afraid to seek professional guidance on how to deal with him or, in some cases, how to leave the relationship.

Can I Tell My Boyfriend to Take Down Pictures of His Ex?

Dear Jess,

My boyfriend and I have recently decided to become exclusive. I realized the other day that he still has pictures of his ex on his Facebook page, and it really bothers me. Can I tell him to take them down? What should I say?

"Tell" is probably not the word you want to use. After all, your boyfriend is probably a grown man, and even his own mother would refrain from commanding him to do something at this point. "Ask" is more fitting in this respect, and, yes, if it bothers you, you can ask him to remove the pictures.

Keep in mind that he may not even realize that those pictures are still on his page. Many people upload pictures, tag their friends, and then never look at them again. Therefore, the first thing I would say to your boyfriend is this: "I realized the other day that you have pictures of (insert name) on your Facebook page. Did you know they were still there?"

See how he responds. He may confess he had forgotten all about them and rush to take them down. Then the conversation is over and you can move on to more important things. However, if he says he's aware of the pictures but seems unconcerned, then you will have to tell him that they make you uncomfortable. Don't drop hints or make snide remarks about the girl. Belittling someone he once cared about will only make you look jealous, and he is more likely to get defensive and stand his ground. You need to be direct in what you are asking of him and genuine in how it makes you feel. Here is what you should say: "I have to be honest with you. It really bothers me that you have pictures of your ex still posted online. I would really appreciate it if you took them down."

If he tells you it's no big deal or that you shouldn't be jealous, do not retreat. If you don't speak up now, you will harbor resentment toward him and the conversation will come up again later, only it will be more explosive next time. Here is what you should say: "I know you think it's no big deal, but I'm telling you that it bothers me. Is there any reason that you should keep them posted online when you know how it makes me feel?"

If your boyfriend is a good, decent guy, he won't want to upset you. However, if he adamantly refuses to take them down, or promises that he will but never follows through, you cannot kid yourself about what sort of man you are dealing with. All these hiccups in a relationship are the real test of someone's character.

If he does not respect your feelings and constantly does as he pleases, you have to consider that he may just be a selfish guy.

A client of mine was dating a man who not only kept pictures of his ex-girlfriend on his Facebook page, but who also made frequent comments on her photos and status updates. Whenever his ex posted a new picture, he would make a funny or complimentary remark, which really made my client uneasy. When she finally expressed how she felt about his constant contact, the guy simply said she was being insecure. When she attempted to communicate how much it bothered her, he stormed out of the room and told her to stop trying to control him. At that point my client realized if she couldn't have a conversation about something like that, she wasn't going to be able to talk to him about more serious issues in the future.

Trying to maintain a fair, balanced, and healthy relationship with a selfish man will be a constant struggle. His behavior has nothing to do with how much he likes you, or if he has feelings for his ex. If he manipulates you into thinking you are the crazy, unreasonable one, chances are he simply puts himself and his needs above yours. This is not an unreasonable request you are making, so if he cannot oblige you, you have to question his character and your future together.

Besides the risk of taking information out of context and creating unnecessary anxiety, constantly perusing the pages of your favorite social networking site could very well be the reason you are single. Social networking has slowly become a national pastime, but it's neither healthy nor productive to be a full-time online specta-tor. Instead of stalking boys or watching all your friends live their lives, get off your computer and go live yours! When a guy asks you about your interests, you want to be able to say things such as hiking, biking, cooking, or reading, for example. No man will be impressed by how many pictures you're tagged in or the number of comments on your wall. Visiting all your friends' profile pages may be fun, but it doesn't serve any real purpose. If you want to keep a guy interested, remember that *you yourself have to be inter-esting*. Spend your free time working on a hobby or passion that enhances your life and makes you more attractive. Take French lessons. Learn to play the piano. Run a 5k. Anything is better than saying you spent the last hour flipping through photos of someone else's trip to Puerto Rico.

Chapter Six

INTERNET DATING

She was a catch on all accounts. The girl sitting across from me was a petite blonde with a killer figure and a gorgeous face. She had graduated from Wake Forest several years ago with her MBA and had gone on to open her own chain of boutique clothing stores. Her life was going according to plan except in one major area: She was single and had been for the last five years. After trying on her own to meet the right guy, she sought me out for help. This was our very first meeting.

"Bryn, why don't we start with your relationship history? Tell me about your dating experiences leading up to where you are right now," I said.

"I've only liked two guys since college, but neither wanted a relationship with me," Bryn started. "I let both carry on for way too long. I would try to go out with other guys, but I really never met any, so I ultimately would end up just falling back into my old pattern and hook up with one of the two. My friends are all in relationships now and don't want to go out as much anymore. They have all met their boyfriends or husbands randomly at bars or other places, but I don't seem to have the same kind of luck," she said sadly.

"Where are you meeting guys now? Are you going out alone or are you waiting until you have a friend available to go prospecting with?" I asked.

"No, I don't go out alone. I would rather sit home all night than go out by myself."

"That's okay. You don't have to go out to meet men. Have you tried online dating before?" I asked.

Bryn looked surprised that I would even ask such a question. "No. I don't think that's for me."

"Why not?"

She took a deep breath and winced a little. "I'm sure you're going to take me for a snob for saying this, but I don't think online dating is for cool people."

"Why do you say that?"

"I feel like if you're a cool person, you don't need to date online. You will meet people when you go out. I just feel like online dating is for . . . well, nerds. Or people who are socially awkward," she confessed.

"So are you saying you shouldn't have to get online because you yourself are cool or because all the cool guys you want to meet won't be on there?"

"Both, I guess."

"Okay, so you think that if you are 'cool,' meaning well put together, nice looking, educated, et cetera, you should be able to meet people easily, is that right? That you shouldn't have to put forth so much effort?"

"Yes."

"And how is that working for you?"

Bryn just smiled sheepishly.

"It's not working for you at all," I said. "It hasn't worked in five years, has it? Guess what, it will continue not to work because it's just untrue, and your perception of online dating couldn't be further from accurate," I told her.

Was It Something I Said?

"You're going to make me get online, aren't you?" she asked.

"No. I don't make anyone do anything. I will tell you what I think is holding you back, and you can decide if you want to take my recommendation or not. Yes, I think we should create a profile for you. Yes, I think you should start actively prospecting on one or two dating sites. But no, I will not make you do any of this. You have to want to make a change for yourself. There are millions of people on these sites, and they are not all one type of person. Millions of singles are dating online and getting into relationships. You have to drop the prejudgment you have, because your ideas on Internet dating are not only wrong, you're missing the possibility that online dating could be your ticket to a boyfriend. Of course, you won't know that until you give it a shot."

Bryn took a deep breath and replied, "I guess I should give it a try."

"Good," I said. "You have a lot to offer someone, Bryn, but unless you make a public service announcement telling men that you are single and available, how would they know how to find you? You have to market yourself, and online dating is the perfect way to do that. Let go of all the false expectations you had about how or where you would meet the right guy. Those thoughts are keeping you single. As you said, your current mentality is not working for you, so I think it's time for a change."

Bryn understood and nodded her head. "Okay, I'll do it," she agreed. "But do I have to put my picture up? I feel like cool people don't put their pictures online."

I sat back down in my chair. It was going to be a long session.

If you are single and not on an online dating site, you are excluding yourself from one of the best resources for meeting people. Admittedly, when dating sites were initially introduced to the marketplace, they did have somewhat of a stigma. Today, however, it's widely accepted and many happy, healthy marriages have resulted from their services. Finding eligible men to date is the hardest part of being single. Why not open yourself up to meeting men through as many avenues as possible?

Yes, usually you do have to kiss a ton of frogs to find your prince, and you may find yourself on more dates than you thought you would ever go on. But in the end, when you find your true love, it will all be well worth it.

After you have found someone that you initially click with, the rest of the relationship has nothing to do with how you met. Until then, however, you will quickly learn that online dating does have a few nuances that make it different from meeting people the old-fashioned way. In the next several pages, we will discuss how to handle these small but significant differences. Who should e-mail whom first? What are the rules of cyber flirting? How do you get him off e-mail and in front of you? Can you ask him out? (Yes! You just have to know how.)

The following are the most frequently asked Internet dating scenarios with detailed advice on how to navigate each one.

What Do I Say in My Profile?

Dear Jess,

You'll be happy to know I am finally trying a dating site. My only concern is what to say in my profile. Do I tell my life story and everything I'm looking for in a partner? I'm not sure how much to reveal about myself. Please help!

As we talked about earlier in the book, you want to tell the story of you in the most colorful way possible (see page 41, *How Much Should I Reveal about Myself on a Date?* for reference). However, an online profile is meant to do one thing: to get a guy interested in asking you out. It's not meant for baring your soul and declaring all your deepest relationship desires. If you met a man at a bar, you would not walk up to him and say, "Hi, I'm a warm, loving person with a quirky sense of humor who's looking for her soul mate, best friend, and equal partner all rolled into one. If that's you, let's chat!" If you wouldn't say it in person, don't say it online. Keep your bio light, fun, and interesting by giving men a snapshot of who you are, while telling them things that they can relate to or comment on to start a conversation. Below are a few ideas:

- How do you take your coffee? What do you eat for breakfast?
- What TV shows are you watching right now? Be honest, even if they are cheesy.
- What are you most interested in: sports, politics, or entertainment?
- What's the last thing you read? (This does not have to be a book. One of my clients wrote, "The ingredients in my energy drink this morning.")
- What's your biggest pet peeve?
- What's the favorite part of your day?
- Are you a dog person? Cat person? Plant person?
- Who do you most admire?
- What do you find to be the most attractive qualities in a man?

These are just a few examples of topics you may include in your profile. Most people eat breakfast or consume a hot morning beverage, so you can begin to spark a connection just over your shared love for breakfast burritos or black coffee. It sounds almost too simple, but that is really all it takes in the beginning.

When it comes to what you want in a partner, keep that part short and sweet. Don't drone on about how you want to meet someone you can trust, who isn't jealous or commitment-phobic. Citing these obvious relationship deal breakers won't ward off the creeps, and the decent men will question whom you have been dating. Instead, talk about some of the less somber "must haves": a positive outlook on life, someone who is family oriented, a good sense of humor, and a willingness to try new things. When you are writing your online profile, you want to write three or four paragraphs, tops, and *The K.I.S.S. Principle* should be guiding your fingers as you type away!

Although you may be tempted to write your profile as if you were posting a job application for a future husband, fight the urge to do so. You will send guys running if you are too candid about your longing to marry and start a family. First things first! Get a date. Get to know each other. Then take it from there.

Why Aren't Good, Quality Men Contacting Me?

Dear Jess,

I posted a profile on a dating site a few months ago, and it seems like a waste of money. Not very many interesting guys have contacted me. I thought this would be a great way to meet eligible men, but instead I'm just getting depressed. Is it me or do other women have this problem? Is it something I'm saying or not saying in my profile?

In a perfect world, your perfect match would spot you across a crowded dating site, fire off a poetic first e-mail, and proceed to court you over Cotes du Rhone wine. Sounds totally plausible, if not highly likely, right? After all, the most advantageous aspect of Internet dating is that you now have one place to look for potential prospects. Sites like Match.com, EHarmony, Chemistry.com, and the like all answer the question, *where do you meet eligible singles?* So theoretically online dating should be like fishing with a grenade. You post a profile and then sit back and let the dates start rolling in, right? Unfortunately, it doesn't quite happen that way, at least not without a little know-how on your part. With a reported twenty-five million members dating off Match.com alone, it's easy to see how little old you could get lost in the online dating abyss. Suddenly, you realize it may not be that there aren't many good guys on the site; it may just be that the guys you would like to date aren't finding you.

With online dating, marketing is the name of the game. You may think you are portraying yourself in the best way possible, but you are probably unaware of some of the key elements that drive foot traffic to your profile.

Here are some solid tips on how to ensure that you yield the highest possible return rate on your online investment.

1. Expand your search criteria.

It's possible that you are excluding yourself from men's searches, or unconsciously positioning yourself at the bottom of their search list, based on information about yourself and your desired mate. Rather than get too specific with who you are and what you want in a guy, try to be as flexible as possible. Yes, you may want someone who is more than six feet tall, with only a five-year age difference between you, but what if the perfect man for you happens to be tall at five-eleven and six years older than you? What if he exceeds your expectations on all other requirements but falls short of one? Would you really pass him up? The more specific you get about what you want, the more you rule yourself out of searches and matches and risk falling through the cracks. If you want more men to choose from (and you do!), stick to your real "deal breakers" but go easy on everything else.

2. Log on frequently.

Many men admit to searching for women based on how active they are on the site. This is especially true on Match.com where, after three weeks, many prospective men basically assume you are "inactive." If nothing else, just log on, click around, and log off just so you can keep yourself current. You don't want to be thought of as out of the game until you really are out of the game.

3. Change your picture.

This is perhaps the most important element in creating a great online profile. Although EHarmony and OKCUPID advertise personality-driven matchmaking, the reality is that most men and women peruse dating sites like an art gallery, stopping only when a certain portrait strikes them. This should tell you how imperative it is to display a really great (and accurate) photo of yourself. Even if you end up searching for men yourself, if a guy doesn't like your picture, he won't even bother reading your message, let alone clicking on your profile.

Check out your competition and make sure you are keeping up with other women in your age range. You may think your pictures are just fine until you click on your neighbor's glamour shot and realize comparatively you look about ten years older and not nearly as captivating. Investing in a professional photographer is *strongly* recommended. You may think your friends are just fine at picture taking, but they are never going to be as good at capturing you in the best light. I cannot stress how important it is to have great pictures. Make sure the photographer gets several head and body shots. It's important to have both; otherwise, men will assume that you are out of shape and hiding what you look like from the chest down. Quality men are much pickier about who they contact online and can easily pass you by for another girl who's not better-looking but more transparent about herself.

If in actuality you are hiding your figure because you aren't happy with your physical form, you have two options. First, you can put off online dating until you get yourself in the best shape possible (which I recommend for best results). Or you can fight the extra ten pounds that the camera will add by wearing dark colors and trying out several different poses to see which is the most flattering. What I would not do is use an old photo from a time when you were in better shape. You will only be setting yourself up for failure. I had a client airbrush her profile picture to look slimmer, and although she was asked out on many first dates, she was rarely asked out for a second. She eventually realized that she was setting her dates up for disappointment by doing this. She took herself offline, lost twenty pounds, and got new pictures. She is now very actively dating.

Some other tips for photo taking: Wear your most feminine ensemble, professionally blow out your hair, and apply twice as much makeup as usual (you may feel like a clown in person but it will look just right on camera). Flashes can easily wash you out, so you have to overcompensate. Standing next to your best friends or coworkers is also a photo flub. Suddenly your height, weight, eyes, and smile are all being compared to the people standing next to you. Do not take pictures with your little sisters, brothers, nieces, or nephews. Some men won't read your profile and will automatically assume that those kids are yours.

If you do have children, you still don't want to display them in your photos. Men are looking for girlfriends online, not instant families. They are not examining your profile with a fine-toothed comb; they are speed-reading through multiple singles. After a long workday and hours spent online, they can easily misconstrue things. The best profiles are simple, straightforward, and stunning.

Can I E-mail a Man I Am Interested in First?

Dear Jess,

I get so many e-mails from my dating site that it overwhelms me. Most of the guys are not even of interest to me. Would it be all right for me to look for whom I want instead? Can I send a man an e-mail first, or must I absolutely wait for him to contact me?

Lucky you, being the toast of the Internet! I know you are swamped with uninspiring inquiries, but let's take a second to be grateful that there are lots of men who are interested in you. It's a huge compliment to be contacted so frequently. Dating sites are real life digitized, and, in real life, the number of men you are *not* excited about will always outweigh the number of men that you are. You can't expect to post a profile and be suddenly flooded with quality guys. You will still have to pick through the lot, just as you would in any other social scenario.

Typically women do not contact men first in person or online, which will put you in the minority. That's a good thing! Men often complain to me about the low return rate they get from dating sites, having to e-mail fifty women to yield one or two responses. How discouraging that must be. Then suddenly you come along and send them an e-mail! If nothing else, you will likely be thanked for just taking an interest.

I would recommend keeping your introductory e-mails short and simple. Remember the *K.I.S.S. Principle.* You also want to approach a man over e-mail much like you would approach him in any real-life situation. If you saw him at a party or some other social event, would you walk up to him and give him your life story and relationship history? No. You would start with an opening line. Yes, you guessed it, an *Icebreaker!* If you notice on his profile that he went to the same school, came from the same hometown, or enjoys the same hobby as you, make a comment or ask a question about it. If you can't find anything in common, look for the most unusual piece of information about him and pose a question to get the conversation going. For instance, if you noticed that he's recently traveled to Iceland, drop him a line asking why he decided to go there or what he would recommend doing if you ever went for a visit yourself.

I would steer clear of winks, flirts, pokes, smiles, and all the other cute yet ineffective ways to show your interest. Those methods of contact are lazy on your part and easy to blow off on his. They also tip your hand and make it obvious that you are interested, whereas using an *IB* still leaves him questioning if you are really digging him or just being friendly.

Be prepared for some men not to write you back, but don't take it personally. They could already be dating someone else off the site, or they may see something in your profile that suggests a difference in your personalities. Keep in mind that people have other things going on in their lives besides Internet dating, so if you don't get a response from someone you e-mailed, don't spend any time wondering why. Just move on to the next. This is a numbers game for now. The more people you e-mail, the more chances you have at finding the right guy. If you e-mail ten guys a week, you should be able to get three or four dates in a month.

Once you get a response from someone you find attractive, you want to make sure your e-mails keep him interested. For more information on that, jump to the last question of this section on page 164, *What Are the Rules When Writing E-mails to Men?*

Why Did He Lose Interest after Our First Date?

Dear Jess,

A really cute guy started e-mailing me. We have had a great time talking—our last conversation on the phone lasted three hours! He told me how beautiful he thinks I am and how he loves my laugh. We had our first date and everything seemed okay, but now I haven't heard from him. I don't understand how he could seem so into me before and now he's disappeared. Should I e-mail him and ask him what happened?

The truth is that although you had good virtual chemistry, it sometimes doesn't translate into a real-life connection. I'm not saying it's all due to a lack of interest on his part, because you seem lukewarm about your first date, too. If it was that stellar, I think you would have described it as better than just okay. Unfortunately, although someone seems good on paper and sounds great on the phone, it's still not enough to ensure that the first date will be a success.

What you have to realize about Internet dating is that in the beginning almost everyone is going out with multiple people. The most probable reason you haven't heard from this guy is because he's recently gone out with someone he's connected with more. Do you need to hear that straight from him? If you do, go ahead and send him an e-mail asking him what happened. You could say, "I thought I would hear from you, but if you've found someone who is a better match, I understand." You can sign it "Just curious" and see if he responds.

Before you actually meet in person, do not put too much stock into what a man says over e-mail or on the phone. Although he may seem interested, you don't become a "real" person until you meet face-to-face. Some men are juggling so many online conversations at once they often forget who they are talking to. It sounds disheartening, but it's the truth, and it should help you manage your expectations a bit better. If you know not to get too excited until you move offline and into the real world, you won't be so disappointed if a date doesn't work out.

Should I Avoid the Phone Conversation and Go Straight for the Date?

Dear Jess,

How do I avoid hour-long conversations? The last man who called me talked for almost an hour and a half!

It's always a good idea to move to the phone for a quick convo, but you don't want to be chewing the fat for three hours with a man you've never met. The purpose of moving to the phone before the date is to make certain you can talk easily. If there isn't a good flow and you are having trouble connecting, then it's a safe bet you won't hit it off in person either (although it's not always the case). The phone can save you the time and energy of getting all dressed up for your date (which usually takes longer than the date itself). However, if you do find the phone banter effortless, great! Limit your conversation to twenty to thirty minutes—just enough to know that you communicate well, but not long enough to exhaust your topics of conversation. If the guy is a bit of a talker and you don't know how to get off the phone that fast, remember to use *Build–Break–Build* to end the conversation. You can say this: "You are a really funny guy, and I look forward to meeting in person. Unfortunately, I have to go get ready for work tomorrow, but it's been great chatting with you and I will see you on Wednesday."

We've Communicated for Months. Why Won't He Meet Me?

Dear Jess,

This guy and I started talking through a dating site a few months ago. Now we talk on the phone, G-chat, and text all the

Was It Something I Said?

time, but he never says anything about actually getting together. All of a sudden I realize two months have gone by. I told him that this is it, I'm going to be in his neighborhood and we should get coffee. He made up some lame excuse and said he couldn't get away! How can he reject me before meeting me?

As we've established, until you actually meet in person, you are more of a fantasy than a reality. This guy knows, however, that once you meet face-to-face, the fantasy is over. I would wager a guess that he was enjoying the attention you gave him and was fearful that it would stop once you laid eyes on him. Although they may be good about hiding it, I can assure you that men have insecurities too and this guy was obviously worried that once you saw him, your virtual love affair would come to an end. Either that or he has a girlfriend—or worse, a wife!

This scenario has absolutely nothing to do with you. You just happened to have met a man who's not courageous enough to come out of hiding.

In this situation, you should not waste any more time chatting. Tell this man if he ever wants to set a date to meet, you will happily oblige. But until then, you no longer will be casually communicating.

Several of my clients have run into the very same situation. This is why I advise not to exchange texts or instant messages until *after* you have met someone in person. Because it is so easy to send a text, you could go back and forth a hundred times before you even have your date, making you "feel" connected to this person whom you don't even know. Unfortunately, there are people online who do not portray themselves honestly. You could easily converse with a married man who's pretending to be single, or with a man twice your age lying about his. There is no way to know who you are talking to until you meet them live in and person, so until that happens, cool it on the pre-date texting.

The reason you are so disappointed is because you've now invested months into this cyber relationship. You would not feel as let down if you had only exchanged e-mails and had one or two phone calls. Please remember that next time you start chatting with an online prospect. Meeting him comes first. Texting him comes second.

Why Did He Ask Me Out for Only Drinks?

Dear Jess,

I recently got out of a long-term relationship and just put myself on a dating site. A guy who I find interesting has asked me out, but he's suggesting only drinks and not dinner. Does that mean he isn't that interested in me? Should I tell him I want to do dinner?

You may be new to the online dating marketplace, but some guys are seasoned veterans. And what most vets know is that you can spend a great deal of time and money going on first dates, with a very small chance of having any of them amount to a second or third. You should not take his drink suggestion personally. This man has not met you yet, and I believe I've hammered home that he has no idea what you are really like. The truth is that drinks are more time- and cost-effective for him. Most men know within thirty seconds of meeting a woman if they will want to get to know her better, and, if the answer is no,

Was It Something I Said?

they would rather not spend the next three hours engaged in idle chitchat. I'm sure you wouldn't either. Go on the date and see where it leads. Even if you don't hit it off, you've lost only an hour of your life, and he's lost only eight bucks for the Merlot you barely touched.

A quick reminder! If you do make a connection on a first date, don't forget to *end at the Height of Impulse*. Far too many women go for coffee and end up hanging out with their date for five or six hours. With online dating, you should limit your first meeting to one or two hours at the most, especially if you really like the guy. Leave too soon and he can't wait to see you again. Leave too late and his impulse and interest will drop!

If We've Been E-mailing for a While, Can I Just Ask Him Out?

Dear Jess,

I only have one complaint about online dating: The guys spend too much time e-mailing you back and forth! How do I get them to just cut to the chase and ask me out? Can I just ask them?

Even though he's communicating from the comfort of his own home (and behind his computer), he still has to muster up courage to ask you out, and it could take quite a few e-mails to do that. Also, because Internet dating is relatively new, most guys are making up rules as they go. Some of them use e-mail as a warm-up. They feel they need to build a small relationship with you before asking for a real date. They worry that asking you out without some e-mail banter is too forward. Heaven forbid they offend you before even meeting you!

The best way to get off your PC (or Mac) and in front of him is to just go ahead and *ask him out*. But before you make a mad dash to your laptop, let me set some ground rules.

1. Make sure he contacted you first.

If you sought him out and e-mailed him first, then he needs to be the one to ask you. No exceptions.

2. Only suggest coffee.

It's the simplest, most non-suggestive date you can propose. Without actually saying it, coffee says, *I'm just asking to meet you to see if there is any chemistry between us.* This is not an invitation to hook up or have casual sex. Lines can be muddled or crossed at a bar, but not so easily at Starbucks.

3. Preface your date request with a reason.

You aren't on e-mail that much, you can't check it while at work, or you just aren't the "e-mailing type." Whatever reason you state is fine, just preface your date request with one of them. This will buffer your assertiveness and protect you from seeming too eager. Here are some examples of what to say:

- "I'm not much of an e-mailer. What do you think about just grabbing a quick cup of coffee next week and seeing how that goes?"
- "I'm not able to check my personal e-mail that often. How about we set up a time to grab coffee next week?"

Make sure you suggest a day that is at least one week in advance. Anything shorter and you may seem too anxious to meet him. If he comes back with an earlier date, that's fine, but let him suggest that, not you.

How Do I Get Him to Take Down His Profile?

Dear Jess,

I've been seeing a man off Match.com for six months, and even though we haven't discussed a relationship yet, I have been sleeping with him. Last week I noticed he had updated his profile, which means he is obviously still looking for women. I was surprised, as our relationship was going so well. He said he couldn't commit after only six months, that he wasn't sleeping with anyone else, but that he didn't feel that he should feel bad if he met someone for lunch. What should I do? How do I get him to stop looking for other women and be with just me?

It does not seem like you are on the same page with this man. He is not ready for a commitment and is going to continue to date other women. So the question is, do you want to be sleeping with him while he is doing this? I would hope not. If after six months of dating you, he still wants to shop around, I'm afraid there is nothing for you to do except let him.

A cardinal rule for online dating: Do not sleep with a man who is still active on a dating site. If you are thinking about having sex with someone you met online, check to see if he's still active on the site before you become intimate.

If he wants to have sex with you and you know he is still checking out profiles, tell him that you are uncomfortable having sex unless you are both ready to commit to each other. Here is what you can say: "Although I like spending time with you, I don't think it's appropriate for us to be having sex while dating other people. If that means we end up being just friends, then I guess that is what we are meant to be. On the other hand, if we want to continue seeing each other, we will have to set ground rules."

Give him some time to think about this. Don't expect him to say much at this juncture, as he may be thrown off guard. He may go home, think it over, and revisit the conversation after some alone time. Hopefully he will realize that he doesn't want to date other women if it's at the cost of losing you. If he doesn't want to make your relationship exclusive, there is not much more you can do to change his mind.

If a man tells you he wants to continue to see you but doesn't want to make a formal commitment, jump to page 187, *Why Does He Say We Aren't in a Relationship?*

What Are the Rules When Writing E-mails to Men?

Dear Jess,

    I communicate a lot through e-mail. The guys that I go out with tend to keep in touch with me this way. Are there any general rules to keep in mind when it comes to writing e-mails to men?

The rules for e-mailing are similar to the rules for texting. You don't want to be too quick to respond or you will give the guy the impression that dating him is more important than anything else in your world right now. Even if you have the kind of job where you sit and stare at your screen all day long, you want him to think you are busy, enjoying a rich and fulfilling life on your own. *Again, it's important to be unpredictable and make him wait for a response.* Wait an hour or two to reply one day and several hours the next. You want him continually checking his in-box for your e-mail, just as you are continually checking for his.

However, as important as your response time is, it isn't the most critical rule to follow. *When* to reply to an e-mail takes a backseat to the *length and content* of your message. This is where most women lose control and forfeit the upper hand.

Rosalyn, a twenty-nine-year-old successful D.C. lobbyist, had a terrible time getting dates. She had been on EHarmony for six months, and although several men contacted her during that time, only a handful amounted to a first date. When she first came to see me, I couldn't figure out her problem. Everything about her profile seemed perfectly normal. I began to think she was truly unlucky in love until I asked to see the e-mails between her and her last date. Houston, we found the problem! The e-mails told it all. Rosalyn wrote two to three times as much as the guy had. She would answer every question in great detail and ramble on about the specifics of her life. This small but serious mistake was all it took to ruin the element of the chase. Guys perceived her wordy, long-winded (and boring) e-mails as a sign of premature attach-ment. After all, who writes that much to someone they hardly know? The puzzle was solved. It was the length and content of her messages that were messing everything up!

It's a common problem with an easy solution. To keep your e-mail length appropriate, you can once again apply the *Mirror*

Theory. If a man writes you an e-mail that is only four sentences, you want to mirror his message with four sentences back. Never write more than he does. You are the one being pursued here; however, if you write more or ask more questions than he does, then you are the one putting forth more effort and, thus, you are chasing him. Even though it's not the truth, it is the perception. You do not have to answer every question he poses to you, especially if it will take you over your word limit. Pick out the most important questions and answer those. Save the rest for when you meet in person. If the questions you have not acknowledged are so imperative to him, he will simply ask them again. Mirror not only the length but also the tone and word choice. If he doesn't use emoticons or exclamation points, be very sparing with yours. Again, you want to ensure you aren't leaving an overeager impression. Don't end your e-mails with "xoxo" if he simply signs his "best." If you keep the *Mirror Theory* in mind with every line you write, you will maintain a balanced courtship until the end.

Some of you may still be skeptical of online dating even after having read this chapter. If you take away nothing else from this, please walk away with these reminders. First, the stigma of Internet dating is a thing of the past. The fear of telling your future "meeting story" should not prevent you from using one of today's best modern dating devices. When everyone is toasting you at your wedding, no one will even remember that you met online. So instead of worrying what people will think, focus on being an inspiration for others to do something productive to find love.

Second, online dating keeps your dating muscles in tip-top shape. You will have ample opportunities to hone your skills with men so that, by the time you find your Mr. Right, you won't come out of the gates rusty. You will be well-oiled and ready to put your best foot forward. Finally, by going on dates with a variety of men, you will be able to better define the qualities you're looking for in a relationship. It's all about trial and error, so embrace it!

Online dating can be the perfect solution to those with little time or little exposure to the local dating scene. If you give it a chance, it can open doors and options for you. If you get discouraged, remember that the more dates you go on, the better your chances are of finding the right person. Who knows, you could get lucky and the next first date could be your last.

Chapter Seven

FINDING COMMITMENT

Lila had been single for almost three years when she met Robert, a handsome entrepreneur from Georgia. They had instant chemistry, and Lila suspected right away that she had met "the one." They laughed constantly, loved all the same things, and shared all the same interests. There was only one small snag: Robert had recently divorced his wife, and she was the only woman he'd ever been with. They had been together since the ninth grade and never dated anyone else. Because of this, Robert felt that he owed it to himself to stay single for a while and experience dating. He was upfront about this with Lila and admitted that he had been out with only two other women since he had been separated.

Lila had been coaching with me for almost two years and knew that she needed to be careful. She was worried about falling in love with someone who wasn't ready for a serious relationship. But as hard as she tried, she fell into a dangerous pattern. She saw Robert three times a week, took down her online profile, and even began spending the night.

At first Lila was okay with their arrangement. Robert was always honest with her and very considerate of her feelings. She didn't think he necessarily wanted to date around, but more so felt he had to because he shouldn't jump into another serious relationship too soon.

And then one day Lila's mentality abruptly changed. Robert was being honored at a conference out of town and she decided to sneak a sweet congratulations card into his suitcase. When she didn't hear from him that night, she sent him a text to wish him good luck. To her surprise and utter dismay, Robert responded hours later with nothing more than a simple "Thanks."

Lila felt like a fool. She phoned me early the next morning with a horrible stomachache. She realized she was in love and the thought of Robert going out with anyone else made her sick. She asked me what she should do. She wanted to be with Robert, but she couldn't take being in limbo any longer.

"What am I doing? I feel like this relationship is one step away from falling apart," she said.

"Here is the problem, Lila. You have stopped letting this man court you. You cannot act as if you're his girlfriend when you aren't yet. You are just dating right now, and when you are at that stage with someone, you should not be hiding cards in their luggage and sending them good-luck texts. That is a girlfriend thing to do, and you are not his girlfriend," I told her.

As if a lightbulb went off, Lila nodded her head vigorously. "I understand. I am not his girlfriend," she repeated. "I guess I'm not used to 'just dating' someone because I've always been in a relationship. What should I be doing?" she asked.

"When you are just dating, you have to let the guy pursue you. You cannot let yourself get too comfortable with him. Once you are actually in the relationship, it's fine to text him good luck and do other nice things once in a while. Until then, you have to refrain from giving too much."

"How can I get him not to want to date other people anymore?" she asked.

"If he really likes you, Lila, and I believe he does, he will not want to lose you. You spend a lot of time together and he's very consistent and open with you. I think if he senses you need more from him, he will give it to you."

Lila knew what she had to do. Up to that point she had been seeing Robert once during the week and then both Saturday and Sunday, far too much time for someone she was "just dating." On the days she didn't see him, she would forward Robert funny e-mails or check in with a quick text. All that had to stop. When Robert returned from his trip and asked her what time they were meeting on Tuesday as usual, Lila replied that she couldn't get together that week. He would have to wait until Saturday.

Lila let five days go by without any contact. She also put her profile back online.

When Friday finally rolled around, Robert told Lila how much he missed seeing her that week. She made a little joke about how she wanted to give him more time to date and get it out of his system. Robert asked if she was serious, and she replied, "Yes, of course. I know what you need to do. Don't worry, I'm continuing to date myself." Robert didn't say anything after that. He sat there pensively for a few minutes until Lila changed the subject to where they were going for dinner.

The next morning Lila woke up in Robert's arms. She and I had talked about how she wouldn't change her routine completely (as that would be too jarring), but she would limit her time with him so that he could miss her more. Realizing that she needed to stick to that plan, she began to get out of bed and get dressed.

"Where are you going?" Robert asked.

"Oh, I just have some things I need to do today. Go back to sleep and we can talk later," she told him.

Was It Something I Said?

Suddenly Robert sat straight up in bed.

"I don't want you to leave. I've been thinking about it all night and I don't want you to date other people. I don't want to date other people either! If I don't take you off the market right now, I think someone else will," he exclaimed.

Lila was shocked upon hearing this. She was hoping that her new way of thinking would change things, but she didn't think it would happen so fast.

"So are you asking me to be your girlfriend?" Lila clarified.

Robert smiled and lifted the blanket for her to get back into bed.

"That's exactly what I'm asking."

If there is one point to hammer home about commitment, it is this: You must not assume the role of a girlfriend before it's been made clear that you are in a committed relationship. When you become a couple, the relationship should be balanced, but until then it needs to be uneven with the man in pursuit of the woman. Although it may be in your nature to do nice things for people and go that extra mile, when you are casually dating someone, you must fight the urge to please. Offering to pick up dinner, help paint his bedroom, or organize his office space are all examples of girlfriend-type tasks. You may feel you are being selfish and inconsiderate by not offering your help, but truthfully you are being very presumptive because you are assuming the relationship too early. Men like to pursue, and even something as trivial as initiating a "good morning" text can end the chase for them.

The journey from "just dating" to "girlfriend" can be a relatively smooth one; however, at times, turbulence may occur. How you handle the twists and turns in this transition period will make all the difference in landing safely in his arms or grounding your relationship permanently. In this final chapter we will explore some of the most delicate dating scenarios and offer suggestions on how best to maneuver them. It's crucial to know how and when to have the "relationship talk" or when to say *I love you*. It's important to know how to tell someone you are looking for commitment, or when the time comes, how to bring up marriage. Below are the most common questions related to commitment with detailed advice on how best to handle each one.

How Do I Figure Out If He Will Want a Relationship?

Dear Jess,

My friends have told me that I have horrible taste in men. My relationships are always tumultuous, and I have a hard time getting the guy to commit. My question to you: Is there a type of guy that I should be looking for and a type of guy I should avoid? How do I figure out if a guy is going to want a relationship with me before getting in too deep?

As we touched on in "What Should I Talk about on Dates?" in Chapter Two (page 37), you want to find out if the guy you are dating has "relationship" qualities. Besides looking for men you find attractive and whose personalities you like, you also need to find out if they are the type to commit. There are some men who are not capable of committing because they possess certain personal characteristics that make having a healthy relationship impossible. These characteristics include the following:

- Tendency toward anger or overreacting
- Selfishness
- Low self-esteem (which sometimes is disguised as arrogance)
- Possessing a victim mentality (nothing in life is ever his fault)
- Recurrent lying or cheating
- Substance abuse issues

Unfortunately, spotting these types of men with the naked eye is impossible. They can be very good-looking and charming despite having these issues, and that can blind you from seeing their fatal flaws. Therefore, you have to ask deeper questions to determine a man's character and then *verify it over time.* Here are a few questions you can ask to help you gain insight into the type of man you are dating and gauge if he will be willing and able to have a normal, healthy relationship with you.

Remember, if you have sex with him before learning his true character, it will be much harder for you to determine his character and much harder for you to walk away from him.

1. Ask him about his family.

What kind of relationship does he have with his mom? How often does he talk to his dad? A man who treats his parents with respect will likely do the same to you. If he displays anger, resentment, and general hostility toward members of his family, there could be deep-rooted issues that need resolving before he can become a good partner for you. Typically, a man will be most him-self around family, so watch how he interacts with them. Given that you are looking for a man to start your family with, how he treats the one he already has will be very telling.

Of course, not everyone is blessed with wonderful supportive parents, so if that happens to be the case with your guy, observe how he treats the closest people in his life—perhaps a best friend or another relative. If he has had a tough upbringing but is still able to cultivate close, healthy, non-romantic relationships with people, he may be one of the exceptions who turned out okay despite his background.

2. Ask about his past relationships.

We've talked about this before, but you want to know details. *You can tell a lot about how someone will act in the future by digging into that person's past,* so ask what his relationships have been like. Was there constant fighting? Was there lying or cheating on either side? He doesn't have to give his ex a glowing recommendation, but if he puts all the breakup blame on her, it could be a red flag. If she really was so terrible, why did he continue to date her? You want to pay close attention to what a man says about his past rela-tionships. Be aware of signs and symptoms pointing to one of the fatal flaws. If he tells you something about a former girlfriend that doesn't make sense, remember to dig further and ask him, "What do you mean?" You want to find out what kind of character he has now, while you're dating. Not in six months when you've already moved in, picked out bedroom furniture, and gotten a dog together. How he treated his last girlfriend is likely how he will treat you.

3. Ask about his pet peeves.

Everyone has them, but you are looking for the good kind of pet peeves. If he's annoyed by people who are rude to waiters or other service people, that is a good pet peeve. It shows he cares about others and treats everyone equally. However, if he says he hates when people don't make eye contact with him or he has a problem with authority, it could be a sign that he overreacts and looks for opportunities to vent his anger. People often show their true colors through adversity. Everyone can be nice and flexible when life is going his or her way; it's when storm clouds roll in that a person's true nature emerges. Instead of waiting months to see your date's character tested, ask him about his pet peeves and you will get a taste of it. Then, if a challenge arises while you are dating, take close notice of how he reacts.

4. Ask about his best friends.

Much like the ex factor, this question will give you a sense of the kind of relationships your guy has with others and, more important, what kind of lifestyle he lives. Normally, as the saying goes, you are who you keep. If all his friends are hard partiers who frequently abuse alcohol or drugs, for instance, it's a safe assumption that he does as well. Then you have to ask yourself the question, do you want a boyfriend you have to chase from party to party? Do you want to spend the majority of your time hanging out at bars and nightclubs? If you are looking to settle down, you are going to need someone who is an equal partner, not someone who requires constant supervision to keep him on the right track. You want to be his girlfriend, not his mother.

If you begin to see that your date is lacking in several character departments, do not ignore the signs. Wasting time with an unsuitable suitor is the number one reason women stay single. Once you realize the guy you are dating has fatal qualities such as a bad temper, drinking/drug problems, deep-rooted insecurity, narcissism, or chronic lying or cheating, do not hold on to the relationship hoping for him to miraculously change into someone else. Find a guy who you not only have chemistry with, but one who also has the qualities necessary for a healthy, long-term commitment. Good, decent, handsome guys do exist!

How Do I Make Sure I Don't Screw Up My Relationship?

Dear Jess,

For the first time in years, I've met someone I like! I'm excited but also terrified I will screw it up. I met him a month ago, and we've hung out a handful of times. We've gone to dinner, the movies, and his work Christmas party. He does contact me a couple of times a week, but I'm not sure what he's looking for yet or how much he likes me. I know I want to be in a relationship with him, so how do I act around him to make that happen?

First off, it sounds like this guy does like you! I don't know what kind of guy he is, so I can't tell you if he's the type who will want a relationship or not, but for all intents and purposes, I am going to assume he's a nice normal man. If he is in fact normal, then any abnormal behavior from you will definitely scare him away. Abnormal behavior, or what men call "crazy," can be categorized a number of ways. In the dating realm, it is usually labeled as one of the following: acting desperate, needy, dependent, paranoid, overbearing, bossy, or controlling. Perhaps you are thinking right now that you are not any of those things. That's good; however, you can also be perceived as crazy if your feelings and actions toward him are accelerated beyond what he considers normal for the amount of time you've been dating.

Some women have trouble appropriately managing their feelings when they first start seeing someone, and they often feel and act as if they are in love after only a couple of dates. If you are guilty of this charge, how then do you stay in control of your emotions so you don't ruin what you've just started? How do you keep yourself from getting attached too soon and combat crazy behavior? The answer is this: If you want this guy to really, really want to be with you, then you must not worry about what the future holds for the two of you right now. You must not stress about when you will see him again or when he will call. You can think and deal with only the date you are currently on right now. *You must live and date in the present.*

When I first met my client Chelsea, I couldn't figure out why she didn't have a boyfriend. She was smart, pretty, and friendly. She met men easily and went on lots of dates, but nothing ever went to the next level. After asking her several questions, it became clear what was holding her back. It was her mentality.

Chelsea was always living in the future. On her dates, her mind would wander. When would she see him again? When would he call? Would he want a commitment? She overanalyzed comments and was easily upset by setbacks. She just could not enjoy the date she was on. Everything was analyzed against the backdrop of the future. As the courtship continued, she would stress more and more about where things were going. These thoughts unknowingly permeated her entire being and, within months, drove all interested men away.

You've been dating this man for only a short time. Therefore you should not be worrying about a relationship just yet. You are still getting to know each other to see *if you will want a relationship*. If your mind is consumed with getting him to commit, you will sabotage your chances without even knowing it. Dating is a "get to know you" phase, and if you can accept that, you will be a lot less stressed and have a lot more fun. When you are with him, don't fast-forward and obsess about what will happen next. Worrying about what he is thinking, when he will call again, or what he is doing is living in the future. How can a man fall in love with you if you are existing in another time? Even if it's just in your head, it will prevent him from truly knowing the real you. Living in the present is the only way to date. If you stay present, the most authentic you will surface and you will not display any of the crazy, negative, self-defeating qualities.

Think about this: You wouldn't go out with your girlfriends and worry about when you will see them again, right? You wouldn't cater your answers, trying to get them to like you more or enticing them to spend more time with you. You have no agenda with your friends other than to enjoy one another while you are together. Once you leave them, you don't think about the next time you will see them or who will call who next. That is the exact same mentality you want with men as well. Be as present with a man as you are with your friends. Still ask him questions to determine if he's the right person for you, but stay in the moment when you do this. That is how you get him to truly want to be with you.

Was It Something I Said?

How Do I Tell Him I'm Looking for a Relationship without Freaking Him Out?

Dear Jess,

Why does commitment freak so many men out? When I tell the men I don't like that I don't want a commitment, they are all over me. When I tell the men I *do* like that I am looking for a serious relationship, they seem to back off. Is there a way to tell a guy you are looking for a relationship but not freak him out?

Let's first tackle why commitment freaks men out. Imagine you are walking through the mall and you see this beautiful dress in a shop window. You think it might be perfect for an upcoming event. You walk in and see that it's quite pricey. It's more than you had hoped to pay, but, if it looks spectacular on you, you could afford to splurge and buy it. As you are about to try on the dress, the saleswoman comes over to you and says, "I'm sorry. I can't let you try this on unless you are going to buy it." Stunned, you think, *But how can I know if I'm going to buy it unless I try it on?*

This is the mentality that guys have toward commitment. They need to essentially "try you on" before knowing if they are going to commit to you, and a couple of dates just won't suffice. To really know if you are a fit, the guy needs to spend some quality time with you first, and that process can take anywhere from six weeks to six months (and you should be the same way!). Like you with the dress, he already likes what he sees, but committing to taking himself off the market is a much bigger step. This is why you have to essentially play it cool when it comes to commitment.

You don't want to be that pushy salesperson, demanding that he make a decision right away. That will only overwhelm him, and he will walk right out the door.

If a guy asks what you are looking for, and the answer is a husband and 2.5 children, there is a right way to say that and a very wrong way. Here are a few rules to abide by when discussing commitment with men.

1. Make sure you speak in broad terms.

"I would like a family one day" is a lot less pressuring than "I'm looking to get married, and I'm not interested in dating someone who isn't ready for that" or "I was born to be a mom, and I hope to have at least five children." The words you choose can make you sound rigid and desperate or confident and flexible. Regardless of how old you are or how much you want it, you do not want a guy to think marriage is your be-all-end-all goal. It will scare him, and rightfully so. Marriage and kids are huge responsibilities, and for a single guy it is a big shift in lifestyle, even if he's excited about it. So keep the commitment comments light.

2. Don't repeat yourself.

Saying it once is enough. Reiterating that you are over casual dating and looking for long-term mating will only make you sound like a husband hunter, and no man is attracted to that. Even dropping hints here and there will put pressure on the guy and could cause him to make a premature decision about your relationship.

Remember this: A man is not going to base his decision to commit to you because it's what *you want*. He's going to commit because it's what *he wants*. So telling him ten times that you want to get married is unproductive.

3. Time it right.

The most appropriate time to talk about the future is when the guy asks about it. The reason: If he brings it up, it's because he's ready to have the conversation. If he doesn't, then it means he's not, and nothing is worse than having that kind of a talk with someone who's not in the same place as you. If you have been dating a guy for more than six months and he has never talked about the future with you, then you will absolutely have to bring it up yourself. For advice on that, move on to the next question.

How Do I Bring Up the "Relationship Talk"?

Dear Jess,

I'm dating a great guy whom I am crazy about. We've been together for several months. He calls when he says he will and always follows through on his word. I have zero complaints for the first time in my life! The only downside is that we have not yet had "the talk." How do I bring that up to him?

Sounds like you may have found a keeper. Good for you! Does he consider you to be exclusive? Are you still dating other people? Can you start introducing him as your boyfriend? These questions can all be answered with one little conversation. But how do you bring it up? Before you cross the Rubicon and have this discussion, you must think this through. Once you have the talk, there is no going back. Say too much too soon and you could scare the guy off. But wait too long and you could lose your sanity or, worse, waste your time on a guy who never had long-term intentions. So what's a girl to do?

First off, you always want to start a conversation like this *from a position of strength*. In this case, you want this guy to be your boyfriend. You want him to stop seeing other girls and make you his one and only. But what kind of bargaining power do you have that will make him want to do this? In other words, what will he get in return that he is not getting now?

When my friend Cara started seeing her boyfriend Justin, she kept herself in a position of strength simply by not spending the night at his house. They would hang out, watch movies, eat dinner, and fool around, but never did she put on her pajamas and climb into bed with him. He hated that she always went home and eventually asked her what he needed to do to get her to stay. That's when they started having the talk. Here is how the conversation went:

> *Boyfriend:* I can't believe you're leaving. Why won't you just
>   stay the night?
> *Cara:* I feel like that is a "girlfriend" thing to do. We are just
>   dating right now, so until we have that talk I don't want
>   to cross that line.
> *Boyfriend:* Okay, so if we have the talk, you will stay?
> *Cara:* Sure. [*She sits back down and waits for him to start
>   talking.*]

Because her boyfriend wanted her to spend the night, Cara was able to negotiate from a position of strength. Once she communicated to her boyfriend that she needed confirmation of their relationship to sleep over (and ultimately have sex), he gladly gave it to her.

In *You Lost Him at Hello,* I talk about *Holding Back Your Bullets* to keep a man interested. Bullets are a woman's valuables, everything from kissing to making love. Bullets can also be a woman's time and attention, which are just as valuable. In Cara's case, time was her Bullet. She would not spend the night until she was Justin's girlfriend. She held that Bullet back until she was certain Justin was ready to commit.

You can decide what Bullets you want to hold back, but make no mistake about it, you must hold back something to have this conversation the right way. Once again, let's remember that until a guy has had the talk with you, *you cannot assume the role of a girlfriend.* You cannot act as if you are in a relationship by having sex, spending the night, or just being constantly available, when you are not yet. Even if you have been dating for several months and feel by this time you should be more intimate, you must hold back *until it is confirmed by him that you are a couple.*

What Do I Do If I Haven't Held Back Any Bullets?

Dear Jess,

What do I do if I've been acting like a girlfriend all along and haven't held back at all? How do I bring up the conversation then?

So you have been going full throttle since you first met. Not only have you been spending the night, but you have also had sex with him, and you are currently communicating on a daily basis. You are now in a position of weakness because you want him to give you girlfriend status but you have nothing that he wants in return (because he's already getting it!). Because he has nothing to gain, you will have to take the opposite approach now and show him what he has to lose.

For things to change, you have to do something different. Doing the same thing over and over and expecting a different result is the definition of insanity. You have to show this guy that you are not getting what you need, and if he wants to keep you around, your needs have to be met.

Option 1:

After you have had a nice dinner and maybe a serious smooching session, give your guy a big hug and say, "This has been a great night (build), but I think I'm going to go home now (break). Thanks again for picking up the takeout (build.)" He will be thrown off at this sudden change in behavior. He may ask you why you are leaving or at least look confused. This is when you tell him that you really like him, but things have progressed a bit fast for you. You feel like maybe you should just slow down a little because at xyz months of dating, you don't know how you feel about the relationship . . . does he? Or you can say you aren't quite sure if you know where this relationship is heading. Then you *sit there in silence and wait for a response.* If he says he thinks everything is fine or gives you some other vague response, don't let him off the hook. Tell him that you feel like you are both acting as if you are in a relationship without actually being in a relationship. Don't say anything more than that. If he gets quiet and has a hard time opening up, give him time to think. Once again, use the silence to your advantage and don't try to fill the void. Your goal is to get him to tell you that you are exclusively dating. If he does not say this, then you must get up and actually go home. Eventually, if he likes you, he will start talking.

Option 2:

For those of you who are completely in the dark about a man's feelings and find yourselves becoming more and more angry, sad, or frustrated by your guy's ambiguous behavior, it may be time to have a very frank discussion. If you have fired off all your Bullets and have been dating for at least six months without a hint of commitment, it's time to lay your cards on the table. Starting with a build, here is what you can say: "I really like you and enjoy hanging out with you. However, I feel like we've been dating for a while now, and unfortunately I'm not sure if this is the right relationship for me. I really need to be with someone who is verbal with his feelings, and I'm getting the impression that is just not you. Please let me know if I am misreading you, but from my perspective it doesn't feel like we are really connecting."

My client Rosalie had been dating Carlo for four months when she decided to have the talk with him. Although she and Carlo had been seeing each other very consistently and talking almost every day, he had not expressed any of his feelings to her. He had never said he missed her or told her how much he cared about her. Frustrated, Rosalie decided that she couldn't keep seeing someone (and hooking up with him) without knowing how he felt about her. She wanted to ask Carlo, "Where do we stand?" However, she realized she had to focus on the fact that she was not happy *at present* and couldn't continue dating Carlo if he wasn't more verbally expressive about his feelings for her. Asking where they stood wasn't going to change the fact that he didn't act as affectionate as she needed him to be. Rosalie also realized that she had been unable to completely be herself in the relationship because there was no emotional communication between them. Rosalie did not want to put Carlo on the spot by asking him questions, so instead she took an alternate approach. She told Carlo what she needed. She made the aforementioned statement and then let the silence take over from there. What did Carlo do upon hearing this? He opened up! He told Rosalie how much he liked her and wanted to try harder for her. He explained he had never been able to truly talk about his feelings with anyone. He assured her that they were exclusive and he didn't want her to give up on him so quickly. Rosalie immediately felt better, and she decided to give the relationship some more time.

If a man hasn't expressed his feelings or discussed commitment with you in six months, it is time to realistically examine your relationship. Either he's not an emotionally expressive person, or he simply isn't thinking about a long-term future with you. Either way, it's time to find out which it is.

What If I Had "the Talk" and It Didn't Work?

You said your piece and he didn't say anything. You couldn't stay after that, so you left and he let you. He hasn't called to ask you to come back, and you are beginning to regret opening your mouth at all. Stay calm. Whatever you do, do not go back on your word. If you are not being fulfilled by a relationship, you must *be willing to walk away*. Give him some alone time to think about what you said. Be patient and let him figure out how he really feels. If you don't hear from him, then you will know that he was truly the wrong person for you. Even if you are sad and felt sure he was the one, you must trust that in time you will see he was not. He may have figured out you were not a good match before you could see it for yourself. A guy who is truly right for you will want to be with you and will come after you. Finding a guy you like is just one part of the relationship equation. The other part is how he interacts with you. It is possible to really like and respect someone as a person but not be able to connect with him in a way you need.

If he does text or call and asks to see you, know that you are back in a position of strength. Your relationship is now equally balanced. Be cautious not to fall back into your old routine. Don't cave and start hanging out with him when nothing has been discussed. He has to meet your needs for you to meet his. Make sure you maintain your stance on what you want; otherwise, you will be right back where you started. If he doesn't bring up the conversation, make sure you do. All you have to say is, "Are we going to finish the conversation from the other day?" If he is serious about you, he will tell you how he feels. If he tries to skirt around the issue again, promptly take yourself home for the second time.

Why Does He Say We Aren't in a Relationship?

Dear Jess,

Recently, my boyfriend of one year told me he was not ready for a serious relationship. Of course I was devastated when he told me this, but then just three days later he called and said he missed me. Now we hang out all the time, but he still maintains he doesn't want to be in a "relationship." The confusing thing is we act no different than we did before we broke up. Should I say something to him or just keep letting him think we are not in a relationship when we really are?

Before I answer your question, let's revisit Chelsea, my client who was living in the future. She started dating someone exclusively, and they went out for several months. However, as it often happens, issues occurred and they eventually broke up. Instead of cutting the relationship off cold turkey, however, she and her ex kept in touch. They said they wanted to remain friends, but eventually they fell back into their old pattern. The difference was that this time her boyfriend told her that they were not in a "relationship." Chelsea just rolled her eyes upon hearing this and thought, *Call it what you want, but this is a relationship.* They spent all their time together, continued sleeping with each other, and even planned a weekend getaway for her birthday. Chelsea thought, if it looked like a relationship and sounded like a relationship, it was a relationship. What she didn't realize, and what I hope you will understand, is that it wasn't that her ex simply didn't like the word "relationship." What he was saying was, "There is no future here. Spend time with me at your own risk."

If your ex is telling you that he doesn't want to be in a relationship but continues to call and wants to see you, do not mistake his selfish behavior for remorse over your breakup. He is most likely finding the transition back to the single life difficult. Yes, even men need help adjusting. And who better to help your ex adjust than the person who has always been there for him—you!

Do the only thing you can at this point: Cut him off. Even though he's physically still around, he's mentally and emotionally checked out. Stating that you are not in a relationship any longer is his way of warning you not to expect the two of you to end up riding off into the sunset together. It's also his defensive strategy if you find out he is hooking up with other girls—"Hey, I'm allowed! I told you we weren't in a relationship!"

I know the hope is that he will change his mind, but the reality is that he's already looking for someone else. He is using you, and you cannot let him continue to do so. Here is what you should say: "I really don't see why we should be spending any time together at this point. You've told me you don't want a relationship; therefore, I have to move on and find someone who does. I hope you can respect that."

He may continue to try to text or call you, and at that point you will have to ignore him. It's not rude to do so because you've already explained your position (which he's forced you into). If he changes his mind and wants to get back together, he knows exactly what he has to say to make that happen because you've laid it out there for him (although I would be a bit cautious if you get back together—after all, he did break up with you once already).

How Do I Get Him to Spend More Time with Me?

Dear Jess,

I'm in love with a man I've been seeing for six months. He's perfect, and we have a wonderful time when we are together. The problem is we get together only once a week, maybe twice at the most. He has a busy job, lots of friends, and plays sports as well. I feel like our relationship is moving so slowly because he's spread so thin. How do I get him to focus more on me? Is there something I should say to him?

Six months and you are spending only one day a week together? There is more at play here than just this man's busy work life and social calendar. I'm willing to bet you also don't communicate with him every day, haven't expressed any deep feelings to each other, and rarely make long-term plans together. Am I right? He may throw you a few compliments and tell you how attractive you are, or how he loves your cooking, but those are not significant signs of love. In this case, you have to observe what this man is *not doing and saying.* You have been dating for half a year. If he was crazy about you, he would have told you by now, and it would have been as he stared into your eyes four or five nights a week. Sometimes it is what a man doesn't say or doesn't do that clues you in to how he is feeling.

I remember when a friend of mine brought her new boyfriend to dinner one night. It was the first time she was introducing him to our whole group of friends. He was slightly obnoxious, border-line rude, and extremely arrogant. At the end of the night, she asked us what we all thought. We looked at one another, searching for something positive to say. Finally one of us blurted out, "Uh . . . he seems to really like you!"

If we had liked her boyfriend, we would have raved about him. We would have told her how much we enjoyed his company, and we would have cited specifics. "He seems so genuine!" Or, "He's so smart and thoughtful!" We couldn't say that, though, because it would have been a lie. The only thing we could think to say that was actually true was, "He seems to really like you." And even that was a bit of a stretch.

I'm going to say to you what your boyfriend won't. He's just not that into you. He is attracted to you, which is why he is still seeing you. He positively reinforces what he does like about you because he wants to keep you around, but to express anything more than that would be lying, and most men don't like to lie. I'm sorry if this sounds harsh, but you shouldn't waste your time with someone who isn't crazy about you by now. It's time to have a heart to heart with your man. Sit him down at a time when you are both relaxed and in a good mood. This is not an attack; it's more of an information-gathering session. Remember to begin the conversation with "I feel" so he doesn't get defensive and to begin in a friendly, noncombative way. Here is an example of what you can say: "I feel like our relationship has stalled, and it's frustrating for me. I like spending time with you and think we get along great, but for some reason I feel like we should be further along than we are. Be honest with me and tell me what you see in store for us."

It's possible that the fear of losing you may wake him up so he can realize he needs to appreciate you more. He may have taken for granted how wonderful you've been to him and how little he's had to do in return. Perhaps you were afraid to ask more of him and so he became lazy in the relationship. If this is the case, you have to vocalize what you want or your unhappiness will grow and cause you to resent him.

On the flip side, he may say he's not ready for something more serious and that he believes everything is fine the way it is. Then you have to ask yourself if this is a fulfilling relationship. Either way, it's time to have this conversation and find out. Six months is long enough for him to know if he wants to give your relationship a real chance or not. He does not need more time, even if he claims he does. Don't merely hold on to the good things he tells you and ignore the fact that he's not committing. Even though you may like this guy, you have to concentrate on what you are really getting out of this relationship. It sounds to me like it isn't very much, and you deserve better.

What Do I Do Now That He Wants to Be Exclusive?

Dear Jess,

The man I've been dating for six weeks just asked me to be exclusive with him. I am over the moon. I have acted so differently in this relationship, and I know that is why he wants to be with me. The question for you is, now that I have him, do I continue to play by the same rules? Do I end my dates early? Do I still wait for him to call me? Can I spend the night at his place more often now?

Congratulations! This is wonderful news. All that discipline you've been exercising has paid off and now you are in a committed relationship. Literary high-five!

Do you still have to practice the same principles that got you to this point, or can you relax now and do as you please? I'll start by saying this is an excellent question. Once in a relationship, most women will kick off their shoes and make themselves right at home. Gone are the days of letting his calls go to voice mail or going home to your own bed. At this stage, most women throw all prior rules right out the window. Is that smart, however? Does it really make sense to act any different once you actually land the guy? After all, what you did before got you to where you are now.

If you completely change your habits shortly following the "commitment talk," your relationship will go from bliss to burn-out in a matter of weeks. Why? Because more than likely one of you will begin to suffer from relationship overload. No matter how much you like someone or how interested he is in you, if you become too engrossed in each other's world too soon, one of you will inevitably begin to feel stifled. *Becoming a couple is a process*

Was It Something I Said?

that takes time. It doesn't just happen the moment you decide to be together. Integrating your lives should happen at a slow and steady pace. (Remember what happened when Arielle and Jeb made their second date a full weekend together?) There must be an adjustment period when you transition from single to couple; otherwise, it will be a shock to both of your lifestyles. Suddenly there is this other person always with you. Even if it feels good in the beginning, it will eventually wear you both down as the novelty starts to fade. The question is, who will be worn down first? To prevent this from happening, the best strategy is to ease into your committed relationship, not jump in headfirst.

My client Alexandra was pleasantly surprised when Davis, her boyfriend of eight weeks, asked her to be exclusive. She was the happiest I've ever seen her, but she was also quite apprehensive. She wasn't sure how to transition into "girlfriend" mode. She was used to seeing Davis only twice a week and letting most of his calls go to voice mail; now she wasn't sure how to act.

The first weekend after they became exclusive, Alexandra spent three days at Davis's house, something she had never done when they were just dating. Spending so much time together felt natural to her, and she began to relax. On the third day, as Davis was cooking dinner, he made the comment that he couldn't remember the last time he spent seventy-two hours straight with someone. Fearing she had overstayed her welcome, Alexandra promptly told Davis she was going to head home to catch up on work. This was a good move on her part, because Davis was clearly feeling a difference in his daily routine by having Alexandra constantly there. Leaving him before that feeling grew into something cancerous was the only way to curtail it. Two days later, after having his familiar world back, Davis was begging Alexandra to come over again. She then realized that although they were now committed, they still needed to maintain their independence. They may have been exclusively dating now, but they weren't married.

Most relationships that start off hot and heavy have short life spans, and it's because women stop doing the things that initially attracted their guy in the first place. I have witnessed grown women completely morph into clingy teenage girls at the first sign of monogamy. Just because you have the girlfriend title doesn't mean you've been given the green light to invade and conquer your guy's territory. Remember that you may be in an exclusive relationship, but you aren't engaged or married yet. It's necessary for you to still do things on your own, without him, and to keep your two living spaces separate.

Yes, you can see your guy more, and yes, you can and should be growing closer as a couple, but you need to do it at a gradual pace. Continue to let him contact you more than you contact him. Return to your home and sleep in your own bed a few times a week. Above all, give yourselves down time, away from each other, after long periods of togetherness. Every couple needs a rest at some point. Just give it to him before he gives it to you!

How Do I Get Him to Open Up about His Feelings?

Dear Jess,

I've been with my boyfriend for more than a year now, and I think he's the one. We are actually moving in together next month. We share a lot of the same interests, such as hiking, biking, and camping. The one thing we are not good at, though, is simply talking about anything serious. He doesn't like to open up and tell me how he feels. Not just about our relationship, but even about work problems or other issues. He just shuts down and zones out. I get so frustrated. Is there any way to make him open up about the important things, or is it true that men just don't like talking?

Let me first dispel the myth that men don't like talking. Yes, there are a few men who don't like sharing their thoughts and feelings, but there are others who are as verbose and communicative as any woman. It really depends on the guy. If your man is not naturally chatty, it can be difficult to get him to talk, especially about personal topics. He may have been raised in a household where you don't talk about your feelings, or he may feel embarrassed to share his innermost thoughts because he doesn't want you to see him as weak. (This is obviously a misguided notion, but some men do think this way.)

Regardless of the reason, here are a few ideas on how you can help get your guy to loosen his lips.

1. Choose your timing wisely.

As a female, when something volatile or exciting happens in your life, how fast are you on the phone with your girlfriends recapping the situation? If the sky starts falling, we like to be the first ones to report it! But all men aren't the same way. Some of them need time to cool down and collect their thoughts on certain situations, especially if those situations are stressful. Instead of interrogating him while he's in the thick of things, wait for the storm to pass and ask him after the fact. Giving him a few hours or even a day or two for the dust to settle will make him less emotional and more apt to open up. You may be chomping at the bit to hear the details, but he may need some time to work up an appetite for talking.

2. Walk and talk at the same time.

Women have made talking a favorite pastime, but how often do you see two heterosexual men sitting at Starbucks just chatting for hours on end? Mark Pollard, international writer and strategist, has some good insight on how men talk: "When guys talk about personal stuff, they often don't look each other in the eyes, nor do they even face each other. They're in the front seats of cars, driving. They're in a pub watching sports. They're playing Xbox. They're fishing. They're doing something they can disappear back into quickly if their man-time gets awkward." This can also work for you if you are dating someone who is uncomfortable talking about his feelings. Try getting him to open up while on a run or bike ride, where he can focus on something other than what he's saying to you.

3. Mix up your words.

Every man hates hearing the words, "We have to talk." Their reaction can be so visceral you may as well have said, "We have your test results." An easy fix, however, is to reword your sentences. Here are some alternative ways to start a serious conversation without scaring him into seclusion: "I was thinking the other day about something. What are your thoughts on . . . " Or, "I have a question for you. What do you think about . . . "

Instead of attempting to prepare him for a three-hour discussion on feelings, these alternate openings sound small and manageable. While they may result in longer discussions, it's better to let that happen naturally than to try to get your guy to commit to blocking off a large chunk of his time just to chat. If he thinks he's in for a long, drawn-out conversation, he's more likely to clam up or shut down, so start small.

How Can I Get Him to Make Plans in Advance?

Dear Jess,

My boyfriend and I have been together for four months, and it's nothing but bliss. However, I've noticed that he doesn't plan out our dates like he did before. Often we don't decide on what we are doing until the last minute, and he usually just asks me what I want to do. How can I get him to go back to actually planning our time together with fun activities and giving me more notice? I'm a planner, and I don't like not knowing our agenda ahead of time. What should I say to him?

The good news is you are in a serious, monogamous, happy relationship. The bad news is that it could be time for you to take over as the social chair. The days of your guy planning out an elaborate rendezvous or even Tuesday night takeout are most likely over. But that is not a bad thing! He's letting you take control. He's happy having you make the social decisions, and his attitude has moved from planned to presumed because he assumes you are going to be around for a while.

I have a client who is a planner just like you. Her name is Hillary, and her personality is so type A that she calls herself "type A plus." When she and her boyfriend hit the three-month marker, he relaxed on the preplanned dates, too. Although they would talk during the week, he would wait until Thursday to start talking about the weekend. The plans always included Hillary (in fact, they practically revolved around her), but she still became increasingly frustrated that he didn't inform her of the weekend schedule days in advance. She didn't just want to know *when* they were seeing each other; she wanted to know where they would be staying (his house or hers), where they would be eating, and what activity they would be doing. When she would try to ask her boyfriend these questions earlier in the week, he would often tell her they could talk that over later. Hillary finally came to me for advice on how to handle this, and I told her that she would simply have to learn to relax more and trust that she and her boyfriend were in a stage where it was assumed they would be spending time together on the weekends. As for the specifics of where they would go and what they would be doing, I told her to practice being more flexible and spontaneous and to look forward more to just being with her man on the weekends instead of what they would actually be doing. If you are with the right person, then anything you do together should be fun.

If you've been dating someone and he has been nothing but consistent with how he communicates with you, as well as consistent with when he sees you, there is no reason to panic now. It's very typical for the guy to plan and organize more while you are casually dating and loosen up once you settle down. You may end up being the one to tell him what the weekend plans are, and that is totally fine. Look up new restaurants online and ask him if you should make a reservation. Find a fun activity and send him an e-mail about it. Just remember that too much planning can be overkill for a new, hot relationship. Every detail does not need to be nailed down in advance. If you know you will be seeing him on the weekend, is it really imperative to always know whose house it will be at or what restaurant you will go to? You are in a relationship now, and although you can't relax on everything, this is one area where you absolutely can.

What Should I Say or Do When He's Upset Me?

Dear Jess,

I really like my boyfriend of five months, but recently he's done a few things that have made me question how he feels about me. He didn't want to pick me up from the airport last time I was out of town because he was too busy. Then he went away and didn't call me for almost a week. There are a few other examples I could give, but my underlying question is, what do you do when the one you love upsets you this way? Do you say nothing and pretend to be happy? I know guys don't try as hard after you are in a relationship, and I don't want to seem naggy and insecure, but this bothers me.

Some women are so frightened of being needy, clingy, or naggy that they repress the need to voice any concerns within their relationships. There is a difference, however, between steadily sweating the small stuff versus expressing your hurt, anger, or disappointment with something contradicting your relationship values. Yes, nagging him to put down the toilet seat for the eighty-fifth time or blowing up his phone when he's enjoying boy's night qualifies as annoying and nitpicky, but pointing out that you feel slighted or snubbed when your feelings aren't considered is a whole different story.

Remember Mona from Chapter Two? Well, she had been dating a man for five months when she began to feel slighted in her relationship. She had not had any complaints about Sam until he received a wedding invite from one of his best friends. It was a destination wedding in Barbados, and Sam had responded that he would be going but made no mention of bringing a date. After a few days of mulling things over, Mona decided she had to have a conversation about it. She was feeling hurt and angry, but instead of letting those emotions lead the conversation, she told Sam she had something on her mind that she wanted to discuss. Here is how she broached the subject, first seeking to understand: "I noticed the wedding invitation from Bill on your table the other day. I also noticed that you responded you would be going alone. Is there a reason you don't want to take me as your date?"

Sam told Mona that if the wedding were local he would have asked her, but because it was away and he'd have to pay twice as much for them both to attend, he decided to go alone. He also told her that he wanted to spend some quality time with his old friends one-on-one.

Mona didn't feel any better upon hearing this. She had hoped her boyfriend would want to introduce her to his friends and jump at the opportunity to spend a little away time with her. This is how she expressed her disappointment: "I have to be honest that I'm hurt by this. If the situation were reversed, I would want you by my side at my best friend's wedding. I think you know I would have offered to help with the hotel cost and other expenses. This makes me feel like I'm last on your list behind your friends and finances."

Sam tried to assure Mona that that wasn't the case, but Mona felt slighted by his decision regardless. She went home shortly after their discussion and sincerely thought about what kind of man she had been dating for the last few months. She wanted to be with someone who put her feelings first because she would do exactly the same for him. After taking a week to think it over, she decided that Sam was not the one for her for several reasons. She broke up with him and met someone else the following month.

In every relationship you will have to pick and choose your battles. You will never date someone who does everything right in your eyes, because no one is perfect. You have to decide then what is worth discussing and what is worth excusing. Perhaps if your boyfriend had been too busy to pick you up from the airport but had called you while he was away, you might have been a little more understanding. But because you have two similar instances working in tandem, both making you feel unimportant, it would be foolish to sweep them under the rug. Your hurt feelings will only fester within you and eventually erupt out of the blue. You must have a talk with your boyfriend before that happens. Here is a good way to approach this conversation: "Recently I've noticed that you and I have been on different wave lengths. I was upset when you didn't find time to pick me up at the airport but tried to be understanding of your work schedule. But then you didn't call me all week while on your trip. Those two instances, along with a few other minor occurrences, have left me wondering how important my feelings are to you."

You have not attacked your boyfriend; you've simply expressed how he has made you feel recently. If he becomes defensive and plays the victim or turns the conversation around on you, know that this is a display of selfish behavior on his part. A man who deflects all problems you have with him back on you is purely thinking about himself. Remember, having a healthy relationship with a man who displays a fatal character flaw is next to impossible.

If your relationship means a great deal to him, he should apologize and resolve to do better or at least explain what has been going on in his head. However, if you have seen this recurring pattern from him, it may be a good time to have a more serious discussion about how you want things to move forward. You don't want to have to constantly remind your boyfriend (or eventually your husband) that your feelings need to be considered. Here is what you can say: "I want to be with someone I have a strong connection with. I want to put that person first and for him to do the same with me. Is that the kind of relationship you want here?"

There is no way to predict your boyfriend's behavior after you talk, but you have now done your part to try to work on things together. From here, it is up to him.

When Should I Tell Him I Love Him?

Dear Jess,

Is there a timeline for telling someone you love him? I've been dating someone for six months, and we haven't said it to each other yet. Should I just bite the bullet and tell him first?

Laying "I love you" on a man first is the granddaddy of grand gestures. Next to proposing, it's the biggest step a person can take. That's why, if you decide that the time has come for you to declare how you feel, you can say it first; however, there is one principle you must abide by, and that is . . . be 100 percent certain he will say it back. If he doesn't, your relationship will be thrust into imbalance, and its survival rate, as Carrie Bradshaw would put it, "has the shelf life of a dairy product. It's going to start to curdle in about a week."

Yes, there is always risk associated with telling someone how you feel, so if you are fairly certain he loves you too, but still have some doubt, I recommend dipping your toe into murky water before you just dive right in. Feel your guy out and see what kind of reaction you get. Instead of saying "I love you," you could say one of the following:

- *I'm starting to fall for you.*
- *I love being with you.*
- *I am really starting to have feelings for you.*

These are still serious statements, but they allow you to gauge his response before committing to the real thing. If he reciprocates with a similar admission, you will have more confidence going that last step. However, if you get an awkward silence or change in subject, you can back off and reassess your plan.

As for a timeline? There isn't a definite one, but those that drop the love bomb too soon usually don't escape relationship fallout. Even if you both feel strongly for each other, if you've only been together for a few weeks, the reality that you don't really know each other yet eventually sinks in and sours things. Therefore, it is always safer to at least wait until you are with someone for several months before verbalizing those feelings. Real love takes real time to grow, so if you are eager to say the words after only a matter of weeks, you may simply be in love with being in love or excited that you have a boyfriend.

Real love means full-on acceptance of the other person. It means putting his well-being before your own. Love is a tough job at times because you have to keep doing it even when you are angry or frustrated with the other person. Most important, it is more about giving of yourself than receiving of anything else. If you are ready for all these things, then you may be ready for those three little words. However, if you just simply feel really, really good when you are with your guy, why not just say, "I feel really, really good when I'm with you" and wait for him to say *I love you* first.

How Do I Get Him to Propose?

Dear Jess,

My boyfriend and I have been dating for four years. I'm ready to get married, but he says he's not. We are both in our late twenties and I feel like we should be engaged by now. How do I have the marriage talk and get him to actually propose?

Typically there are two reasons that men don't propose, as long as you are not dating someone who possesses one of the fatal character flaws. If you are dating someone who is selfish, for instance, it won't matter if you look like Rachel McAdams and cook like Martha Stewart. If your guy is of the selfish persuasion, he won't marry (at least until he realizes he's running out of options and may die alone). But if your man has been a model boyfriend, there are only two things that can stop him from getting his knee dirty: Either the timing is wrong or the relationship is wrong. When the timing is wrong, it's typically because the man isn't financially in a position to get married. Buying a ring, planning a wedding, and paying for a honeymoon are just the initial expenses. Then there is buying a house, paying a mortgage, having kids, and so on. You may think that love is enough to propel two people down the aisle, but I assure you, if your boyfriend is a smart man, he is thinking of a lot more than just how he feels about you. Remember, for guys especially, starting a family is a huge responsibility.

Unless, of course, your guy is settled, stable, and spending all his money on his sports car and Swiss watches. If it seems that your guy has the means to propose but maintains that he's not ready to take that step toward lasting commitment, it could be because he feels like your relationship won't last the test of eternal time.

My client Hadley had met her boyfriend Trey right out of college. She was twenty-two; he was twenty-eight. They met at an engagement party for a mutual friend and ended up going on their first date a week later. Trey looked good on paper. He graduated magna cum laude from Princeton, had a great job at a prestigious law firm, and came from an affluent family. Hadley worked on Wall Street, made a great living, and owned her own apartment on the Upper West Side. After four years of dating, Hadley realized that all her friends were getting married, and she felt that she and Trey had been together long enough to take that next step, too. However, when she approached Trey about it, he waffled a bit and told her that he wasn't ready to have this conversation yet. Hadley decided to give him a bit more time and felt good because at least he knew that she was now thinking about their future and wanted him to do the same.

Six months later and with no ring in sight, Hadley decided to bring up the discussion again. Trey told her this time that he was not ready for marriage. Hadley then asked him what would need to be different for him to feel ready, and Trey responded that he didn't know. When she followed up with a second question of how much more time he needed to feel ready, Trey responded, "I'm not sure when I will be ready."

Hadley was devastated upon hearing this and told Trey that after four and a half years together, she needed to move on and find someone who wanted the same thing she did. As hard as it was, she left Trey and put herself back on the dating market.

Four months after she left Trey, she met someone at work and started dating him. She tells me now that leaving her four-and-a-half-year relationship was the best decision she ever made. Although initially devastated by the breakup, she says she is now truly in love and realizes that Trey was not the man she was supposed to marry.

Because you have been together for so long, it is definitely time to have a serious conversation with your boyfriend and figure out what exactly is stopping him from making you two official. Here is what you should say: "We've been together for a few years now. What do you see in store for our future?"

The answer you are looking for is "marriage and kids." If he says he is not sure or isn't ready to take the next step, move to the next question: "When you say you aren't ready for marriage, what needs to be different for you to feel that you are?"

If he says he doesn't feel like he's old enough or doesn't feel like he's mature enough that could be an indication that he has doubts about your relationship (unless he is twenty-two and, in that case, he's probably right about not being old enough). A man of appropriate age who does want to marry you but needs more time to prepare for the responsibility *will tell you exactly that.* He won't be vague and skirt the issue. He will reassure you of his intentions even if he cannot move forward with a proposal just yet.

If you get an ambiguous answer, or he tells you that he just wants to be in a different place in life when he gets married, move on to the next question: "Realistically, how much time do you think you need to feel ready?"

If he can answer this question with a time frame, take it as a positive sign. Even if he says he needs one more year, it means he's aware of what he needs to do and is intentionally working on getting to his end goal. If he stammers, stalls, or, worse, turns the whole conversation around on you, be aware that marriage is probably the last thing on his mind and it could be time to break out the ultimatum.

If you have been with someone for several years and he has not broached the subject of marriage, you will have to be the one to do it. You cannot and should not date someone for years, hoping that one day he will pop the question out of the blue. It does not happen that way. Men who think about marriage talk about marriage. They want to know your thoughts and feelings on the matter. If you are not hearing much about marriage, chances are there is a reason. Once you bring it up, his answer or lack of one will tell you most of what you need to know. If he doesn't give you a definite timeline or reassure you that you are going to be in his future, you must walk away from the relationship. Walking away will answer the question of whether it is the wrong time or the wrong relationship. If it's the wrong time, your boyfriend will come after you. He will not let his fear of commitment, getting older, repeating his parents' mistakes, and so on allow you to walk out of his life. However, if he thinks this relationship can't go the distance, he will let you go. As hard as that will be for you at the time, it will be the biggest favor he ever does for you. It will allow you to continue your search for your true partner in life.

Clients often ask me how long you should date someone before getting married—or how long is too long. The answer to this question really depends on your age and circumstance. If you start dating someone in college, you will most likely date longer before discussing marriage than two people who begin dating in their late twenties or thirties. It's safe to say that the older you are, the less time you need to date, because you both should have enough experience to know what it is you need to make a relationship work. If you are in your early twenties, dating four or five years is not uncommon or abnormal. However, if you are approaching thirty, you don't want to wait that long to talk about the future. Time becomes more precious as we age, so after dating a year or two at the most, you and your significant other should be having candid conversations about the future.

Getting to commitment is, by far, the most difficult aspect of dating. Simply attracting a man is not enough to obtain and sustain a relationship with him. He may like what he sees, but to enter a serious monogamous relationship, a solid connection must be formed. How do you go about forming this connection? Ironically, it all begins with your own feelings about yourself. If in your own mind you worry that you are not pretty enough, not slim enough, not smart enough, or simply not good enough, you will always have trouble moving from casual dating to commitment. Those negative thoughts and serious self-doubts permeate your being. They affect your attitude, your words, and your actions, which can cause you to severely mishandle situations and inevitably drive men away.

Was It Something I Said?

Belief in oneself does not come overnight. It is acquired through time and takes constant effort. Learning how to handle your relationship is realized along with this. I encourage those of you reading, if this sounds like you, instead of primarily focusing on men, concentrate on yourself. It may be time to go back to the basics. Knowing and being your best self will make all complicated relationship situations easier to maneuver.

Chapter Eight

ALL THE RIGHT MOVES

You have now been armed with an arsenal of tactics to help you better communicate in your relationships. You have learned the power of *Feel-Felt-Found* and the effectiveness of *Build-Break-Build*. You understand the importance of *The K.I.S.S. Principle* and see the value in applying the *Mirror Theory*. Knowing these techniques, however, is only half the battle. Reading them as they relate to someone else's situation is very different from applying them to your own life. No doubt you picked up this book because at times you are fearful of making the wrong move in your own relationships. But the question is, now that you have the know-how, will you be able to truly use what you have learned?

I tried to cram as much as I could into these pages. There is little doubt, however, that you will come across your own unique set of circumstances not covered within this book. Then it will be completely up to you to apply the advice given when and how you deem necessary. Although you may be nervous to trust your own judgment at times, let me assure you of one thing before you put this book down and continue your pursuit for the right partner: Men are attracted to women who, above all else, value and respect themselves, and the only way they can gauge how much you think you are worth is by your actions toward them. If a guy does something that hurts you or makes you angry or uncomfortable, know that he will respect you more for standing up for yourself and appropriately addressing the problem than if you give into your fear and insecurity and decide to simply do nothing.

When you begin dating someone, the promise of a new relationship can be so desirable it may create anxiety within you. You might worry that if you rock the boat, you risk sinking it altogether. Or you may believe that there is a perfect response for every situation, but because you have not figured it out yet, you should just remain silent. However, in most cases of relationship turmoil, doing nothing is the most dangerous move you can make. You do need to be flexible and understanding at times, and you can't expect a man to always do and say the perfect thing, but *when something feels wrong and especially if you feel undervalued,* you must address the issue. If, for instance, a man repeatedly says he will call but rarely follows through on that promise, you should react in some fashion. Whether you choose to express your disappointment directly by confronting him or indirectly by pulling away, the choice is up to you. You, of course, do not want to overreact, but to not react at all would send the message that you are fine with his behavior. To continually be fine with him letting you down would, over time, create imbalance in the relationship. But, more important, it would communicate your lack of self worth—and nothing is more unattractive than that. Merely holding on to the hope that a problem will miraculously solve itself is a fool's dream—and you are no fool. You have the smarts and the power to get the loving relationship you deserve, and now you have the tactical prowess to do it. It may feel like you will have to carry this book in your handbag for the rest of your life right now, but there is a way to give yourself the strength and confidence needed to always make the right move.

How to Determine the Right Move

The right move is subjective. What you consider unacceptable dating behavior, someone else may find acceptable. Things that you would let slide may be important to someone else. So how you would react in a situation is not always how someone else would react. That is why advice from others can be so confusing and can often leave you wondering if you are, in fact, doing the right thing. But, don't despair; there is a way to be certain you are making the right move *for yourself.* The secret is to stay true to yourself and *always act in accordance with what you want in a relationship.*

Most women have only considered what they want in a man, right down to his height or income level, instead of what they actually want in a relationship. What you want in a relationship specifically points to the rapport between you and your partner: the respect you have for each other and the connection you share. All this is far more important than checking off whether or not a man fits your "resume" requirements. Everyone has different ideas about how a relationship should function, and only you know what will be best for you. It's time to let go of your list of must-haves in a man, and instead create a must-have vision for the relationship you want with your partner.

Creating Your Vision

Close your eyes right now and imagine your future home. Imagine it is a weeknight and you are just getting off of work. You are tired and ready to kick off your shoes and relax on your couch for a bit. Then, your future husband walks through the door. What is the first thing he says or does? Does he say hello to you over his shoulder, walk to the kitchen, and throw back a beer? Or does he make a beeline to you, scooping you up for a big bear hug? Does he ask you what you feel like doing for dinner? Or does he tell you he's headed out with the guys and he will see you a bit later? Do you sit down and talk about your day, or do you both zone out to the TV until bedtime? What are you talking about right before you sleep? What is the first thing he says when you wake up? Imagine the day-to-day interaction between you and your husband, because this vision is what you are striving for. It is vitally important to create this vision and keep it with you at all times. When you meet someone new, or when difficulty arises within your current relationship, measuring your reality against this vision will help you decide what moves to make.

If you have never thought about the type of relationship you want, then creating your vision may take some time. Personally, it took me a few years to figure out my vision. It changed quite often as I dated different men, but by the time I was thirty, I had it down in my mind. I knew I wanted to be with someone who made me feel special. I wanted my future husband to look at me with love. I wanted us to talk until the sun came up and laugh about the silly things life threw our way. I wanted us to hold hands wherever we went and to always listen to each other when one of us had something to say. I wanted him not to walk away when we fought, because I would never walk out myself. I wanted us to be best friends, to respect each other, and to hold each other to a higher standard than we had for ourselves.

When I started dating my husband, I knew almost immediately that he was someone who perfectly fit my vision. The way he was with me was exactly how I always dreamed being married would feel. He was also handsome and smart (which never hurts!), but I had already met other guys with brains and good looks. It was his good heart, his strong character, and his self-assuredness that allowed him to love me the way I needed, and it was the easy, loving rapport between us that made him the right person for me. No other relationship had ever come close to my vision.

That isn't to say that we didn't have our share of disagreements. To grow as a couple and foster that ideal relationship, we had to have a few contentious conversations while we were dating. When one of us was upset, we vocalized it. We got it out in the open and we worked through it. Had we simply stayed quiet when one of us was hurt by the other, there is no doubt in my mind we would have a very different relationship today—or no relationship at all!

Creating your vision is critical when you are single, for not having one will let ill-suited men slip through the cracks and set your happy future askew. Have you ever known anyone with a lousy husband? Have you ever thought, *How could she marry him?* Or even worse, *Why?* For some women finding the right type of guy is more important than finding the right relationship. A woman may be enamored with a man who seems ideal from the outside but whose values and character are a total mismatch to hers, causing strife throughout their entire marriage. These are the women who, in the beginning, place more importance on landing the guy they fixated on from the get-go than on actually finding real love. They may focus more on material attributes: how tall or handsome he is, where he went to school, what he does for a living, the kind of clothes he wears or car he drives. If you are more concerned about what you will be *getting* from a man—a certain lifestyle or a boost in your own social status, for example—your intentions are in the wrong place, and you will ultimately end up in one of those lousy relationships yourself. If you want a happy relationship, first and foremost, you must simply seek a real connection to someone. Strip out all the enticing but irrelevant influences and focus on how you and that person treat each other on the most routine of days. Then the question to ask is, "Can I cast this person into my vision?"

He Fits Your Vision . . . Some of the Time

Maybe you are with someone right now whom you are crazy about. Maybe half the time he's everything you've ever wanted. He's sweet and charming, affectionate and fun. He makes your heart flutter, and you feel ten feet tall when you are with him. The other half of the time, though, he's cold and distant. Or he makes you feel needy or crazy. Perhaps he's unpredictable, which is what keeps you so interested but also prevents you from truly getting intimate. You want the relationship to work out more than anything, so when he hurts you in some way or lets you down—either intentionally or unintentionally—you resist the urge to say something.

But you are doing this man no favor. By allowing any man to treat you poorly or constantly disappoint you, you are nurturing the worst in him. Whatever it is that bothers you now will only grow and worsen over time if you don't address it. Relationships can be wonderful if both people involved are honest about what they want and need. If you keep quiet and pretend you are happy when you aren't, your relationship will slowly become a nightmare for you both. Couples who are coined "good together" are not labeled so because they simply match up well. They are also honest with each other and hold themselves to high standards. If one gets out of line, the other will not hesitate to provide a reality check. It's not fun to do so, but, much like raising children, if you don't set boundaries for your partner, you will turn him into a spoiled child. No man will love you for that.

But Visions Are Perfect and Relationships Are Not

Perhaps you are thinking, "But nothing is perfect, and I can't hold a real relationship to an imaginary standard." It is true that relationships don't always sail smoothly. Couples have fights. They get frustrated and annoyed at times. When you are creating your vision, you will most likely focus on the ups instead of the downs. That is okay, because a healthy relationship will have many more highs than lows. A healthy relationship can be compared to the weather in San Diego. It's typically warm and sunny year-round, with infrequent bouts of bad weather. Your reality should measure up to your vision about 85 percent of the time. If your relationship feels more like you are living in Miami (it's hot and steamy, but lots of storms) or Seattle (always rainy), your relationship is most likely not living up to its full potential. You should not pretend that nothing is wrong or tell yourself this is just simply how men behave. Something needs to change, and that change will not happen without your initiative.

As you've read in this book, conflict does not have to be a bad thing. While it may be uncomfortable at times, working through problems with your guy should get your relationship to a better place in the end. You have to put in the work, but the reward will be well worth it. Understandably, you may fear that by standing up for your wants and needs, you may risk losing your relation-ship altogether. But the key word here is fear. You cannot be afraid of things ending badly. Instead you must think of the good that is to come! You can be extremely fulfilled and happy if you stay true to your vision. This is what you must tell yourself in times when you are scared to make a move. If you constantly ask your-self the question, *should I be upset with him or not,* or *should I talk to him about this,* then crafting your vision will help you find the answer. If you debate about bringing an issue to light, or if you wrestle with walking away, focusing on your vision will give you the strength to do *something* instead of nothing. In some instances, leaving the relationship will be the right option, but in others you may be able to help you and your partner self-improve. The only way to ensure a happy ending for yourself is to stick up for your vision and make a move toward achieving it, even if at times it means moving away from your guy.

You may feel like you're a world away from happily ever after, and the decisions discussed here couldn't be further from your current life. But any happy ending starts with a first date. Knowing where you want to go from there will help pave the road for a smoother ride. Date with the confidence of knowing what you are looking for, and use this book as a guide along the way. Whether you are in a committed relationship or trying to lock one in, you can be more in control of your future. The next time you freeze and wonder if you are making the right move, go back and consult your vision. Your vision will never mislead you.

Acknowledgments

Writing a book is not a goal you can reach on your own. Without the help of several wonderful people, this book would never have made it to print.

First and foremost, I am exceptionally grateful for my ever-supportive husband, Erik. His love, advocacy, and counsel allowed not only the creation of this book, but the opportunity for me to tirelessly pursue my dream of helping people in my own small way. Erik, I love you and thank you.

Second, I must give thanks to all the amazing clients I have worked with during the last six years—especially my regulars (you know who you are). You may think you are learning from me, but every day I learn from you. You are all so impressive and inspiring to me.

Thank you to my agent, Jessica Regel, who championed this book when it was still merely a concept, and who endured with me the ups and downs of getting it published. Thank you for your solid input and sincere encouragement.

Thank you to my publisher, Globe Pequot Press, and to my editor, Lara Asher. Working with you has been an absolute joy. Lara, you and I are a match made in literary heaven! From fine-tuning the manuscript to working on the title and cover, your collaboration has been critical to this project.

Last, to the McCann-Ballagh family, I am always grateful and touched by your love, enthusiasm, and support in all my endeavors. And a special thanks to Jordie for being the perfect cover model!

About the Author

Jess McCann is an internationally known and recognized dating coach and author of the book *You Lost Him at Hello: A Saleswoman's Secrets to Closing the Deal with Any Guy You Want*. The book was published in ten countries, including mainland China, Taiwan, India, and Indonesia.

Jess began her coaching business in 2007. By the following year, she was receiving dozens of advice-seeking e-mails a day, and her client list was growing exponentially. Today her daily clientele consists of men and women ages 19 to 67, residing in cities all over the world. When not coaching, she continues to spread her message by guest speaking at women's rallies, college campuses, and lifestyle events. She also writes her own blog on www.jessmccann.com. In addition, she is a regular guest on ABC's *Let's Talk Live* in D.C. and is asked to regularly weigh in on segments for ABC's local news affiliates.

After her first book was released, Jess appeared on several national shows, including *Good Morning America*, *The Fox Morning Show with Mike & Juliet*, and *Extra*. Her book has been featured in the *Washington Post*, *Cosmopolitan Magazine*, the *San Francisco Chronicle*, *Woman's Day*, *Essence*, *MSN*, *The Capitol File*, and *Washington Life Magazine*.

Before becoming a dating coach, Jess was a top producing salesperson and owner of her own sales company. She received many awards and enjoyed continued success due to her strong ability to read people, build rapport, and handle objections. She parlayed her business acumen into her first book, teaching women how to use the same skills in the dating arena.

In 2005 Jess was chosen as one of the country's top entrepreneurs and appeared on the reality show *The Rebel Billionaire* with Richard Branson.

Jess married in September 2010, and she attributes finding her husband to using and following her own dating advice. She and her husband currently live in the Washington, D.C., area.